DISCOVER THE POWER OF YOUR IPHONE 14

A COMPREHENSIVE GUIDE FOR USERS OF ALL LEVELS- SIMPLIFYING TECHNOLOGY FOR A BETTER EXPERIENCE WITH LARGE PRINT AND ILLUSTRATIONS

RON BEHRMAN

CONTENTS

INTRODUCTION

When Apple Inc. unveiled the first iPhone in January 2007, everything changed forever. This groundbreaking tool created an entirely new manner of interacting with others, and those who owned it immediately grew to regard it as a status symbol. The iPhone has improved over the years with new features and technology added, going from being merely a mobile phone to becoming a necessary tool for daily living.

But as more functions have been added, it has gotten harder to figure out how to use the iPhone to its fullest potential. Even the most seasoned users may feel overwhelmed and puzzled by the frequent upgrades, revisions, and updates. Herein lies the value of this work.

It's likely that if you're reading this, you've recently purchased or received a new iPhone, perhaps for the first time. You might be eager to learn how to utilize it, but you might also feel a little scared by the idea. It's not just you. This is the situation that many people find themselves in, which is why I wrote this book.

My observations of people struggling to operate their iPhones served as the impetus for writing this book. I've observed a lot of people having trouble using all the features and capabilities of their gadgets. With over 50 years of expertise in the IT sector, I was confident that I could be of assistance.

This book is meant to serve as an in-depth guide to using your iPhone. You can use the shortcuts and advice in it to make the most of your gadget. The living Mapping Method, which focuses on classifying various aspects and functions according to their advantages in daily living, is at the heart of this book. The topics covered in the book are: personal help, remaining safe and secure, interacting with loved ones, obtaining information, improving productivity and enjoyment, and monitoring health.

The knowledge I am providing in this book is the result of years of experience and research. The objective is to make you an expert iPhone user and even teach you stuff that many "experienced" users are unaware of. You will be a part of the more than one billion-strong Apple ecosystem by reading this book.

You will be able to use your iPhone more effectively and easily after reading this book since you will have a better grasp of it. You'll be able to utilize your device's features to their fullest and feel comfortable exploring all of its numerous features and functionalities. The Life Mapping Method can also be used in other aspects of your life, which will enable you to better prioritize your tasks and manage your time. If you are an elderly person, this book will provide you with an iPhone experience that will simplify and make things easier and more accessible for you.

Due to my significant background in IT, I would be an appropriate candidate to lead you through this process. I have spent years assisting individuals in overcoming the difficulties they encounter while learning to utilize technology, so I am aware of the difficulties that people may encounter. I'm sure that this book will enable you to carry out the intended outcome.

To get the outcome this book promises, it was difficult before the initial iPhone was released. But it is feasible if you have the appropriate information and direction. This book will assist you in making the most of your iPhone's features, which will improve your quality of life.

If you want to master the use of your iPhone, this book is for you. Your life will be more productive, and you'll be able to use all the features and functionalities of your gadget with its assistance. You may efficiently prioritize and manage your time by using the Life Mapping Method in other aspects of your life. So let's start now.

1

MAKING YOUR IPHONE YOURS

This chapter focuses on customizing your iPhone to match your personality and lifestyle. It provides instructions on configuring and optimizing the device's features, such as customizing wallpaper, audio, and vibration settings. The chapter also discusses setting up and modifying the control center for increased productivity and efficiency.

Its goal is to help readers gain greater control and comfort with their device, enabling them to use it to its fullest potential. Overall, the chapter offers helpful suggestions and ideas for iPhone users of all skill levels to personalize their devices.

SETTING UP YOUR IPHONE FOR THE FIRST TIME

We're glad you're here, iPhone world! You might be unsure about how to first set up your brand-new device as you unbox it. We've got you covered, so don't worry. In this chapter, we'll take you step-by-step through the setup of your iPhone so you can start taking advantage of all the fantastic features it has to offer.

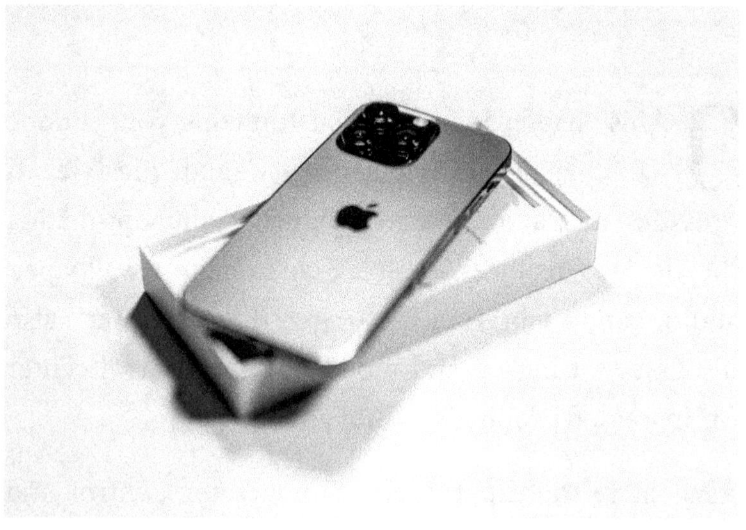

Let's start by looking at the setup requirements. You'll need your previous phone on hand if you're replacing an older iPhone. This is so that you may transfer all of your data, settings, and apps from your old phone to your new one during setup. As a result, you won't have to set up your new phone from scratch and can get started with it more quickly.

You'll also need a SIM card, a tiny chip that enables your phone to connect to a cellular network, in addition to your old iPhone. You won't need a physical SIM card if you have an iPhone 14 or later because it uses an eSIM instead. The phone comes with an embedded digital SIM card (eSIM), which you can activate through your carrier. This eliminates the need for you to physically insert a SIM card into your phone, which is good news. To confirm whether your iPhone has an eSIM, you can check the Apple website or contact your carrier. We'll provide separate instructions on how to install and activate a physical SIM card on your iPhone at the end of this section for those who do require one.

Your Wi-Fi network information is another essential component that you'll require for the setup. You must join a Wi-Fi network while setting up your iPhone in order to finish the process. This guarantees that, throughout the process, your internet connection will be strong and safe.

And lastly, you'll need your Apple ID information. You log in to all Apple services, including the App Store, iCloud, and Apple Music, using your Apple ID. Don't worry if you don't have an Apple ID; you can create one during setup. To use it as your Apple ID, be sure to keep an email address close at hand.

Let's get started on setting up your iPhone step by step now that you are aware of everything you will require. If applicable, we'll begin by moving your information from your old phone. Next, we'll set up your Apple ID, connect to Wi-Fi, create or sign in to it, and configure any optional features like Face ID or Touch ID.

Before we begin, make sure your iPhone is fully charged or plugged into a power source. By doing this, you can prevent your phone from running out of battery during setup, which could lead to issues. We advise sitting down in a quiet area with your iPhone in order to complete the setup procedure at your own leisure.

TURN ON PHONE

The first step to starting is turning on your phone. We will lead you through the process of turning on your phone in this guide.

First, find the iPhone's power button on the right side. While you wait for the Apple logo to appear on the screen, keep holding down the power button. This could take a short while.

Your iPhone will start to boot up after the Apple logo appears. Depending on the model of your iPhone, the process could take a while.

Choose your language and location next. Your iPhone will ask you to select the area and language that best fit your needs. The language used in menus and prompts, as well as the time zone settings, will be determined by this selection.

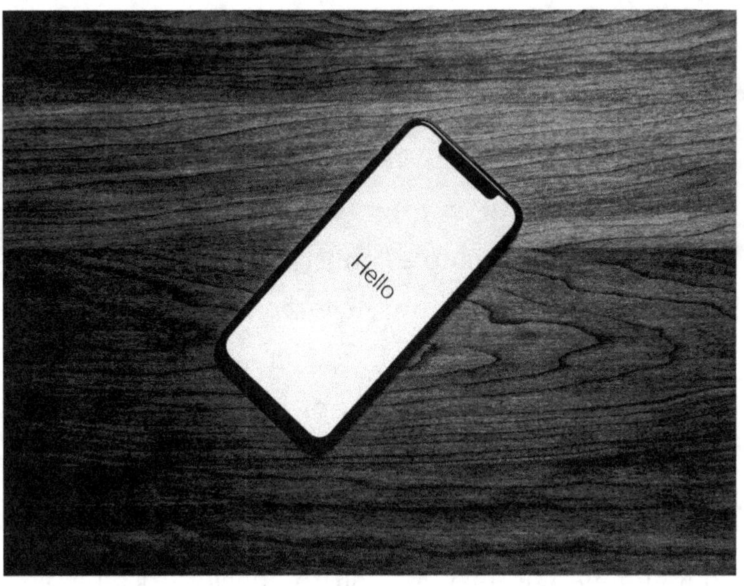

After selecting your language and location, a Wi-Fi network joining prompt will appear. You must choose the Wi-Fi network and input the password to connect. You can forgo this step and connect later if you don't have access to a Wi-Fi network.

The next step is to set up Touch ID or Face ID on your iPhone. You may use your fingerprint or face to unlock your phone thanks to these cutting-edge security features. Follow the on-screen prompts to scan your fingerprint to activate Touch ID. Follow the on-screen prompts to scan your face to activate Face ID. This step can be skipped if you choose to set it up later.

After Touch ID or Face ID is set up on your iPhone, a passcode setup prompt will appear. A passcode can be used to safeguard your phone and prevent illegal access. A six-digit, four-digit, or alphanumeric passcode is your option.

Your iPhone will now prompt you to sign in using an existing Apple ID or to establish a new one. You need an Apple ID in order to utilize the App Store, iCloud, and other Apple services. If you already have an Apple ID, enter your login and password. If you don't have an Apple ID already, simply follow the instructions on the screen to create one.

Your iPhone will prompt you to enable Siri after you log in with your Apple ID. With the aid of Siri, you can perform operations like placing calls, sending messages, and setting reminders. Siri may always be turned on or off in the settings.

Finally, a popup to set up Apple Pay will appear. You can use Apple Pay on your iPhone to make purchases. Apple Pay can be configured in the settings now or later.

Congratulations! You've just finished setting up your iPhone and turning it on. You are now prepared to use your new smartphone.

Manual Setup Process

You've got a new iPhone; congratulations! To get you utilizing your phone as soon as possible, we will lead you through the manual setup procedure in this guide. We will go over each stage of the configuration process and what to anticipate on each screen. Let's get going!

Step 1—Hello screen: The "Hello" screen appears on your iPhone 14 as soon as you switch it on. You will start the setup process for your phone from this screen. To select your chosen language on this screen, swipe left or right.

Step 2—Select a language: On the "Select Your Language" screen, you can choose from a list of available languages. To continue, choose your favorite language and click "Next" in the top-right corner of the screen.

Step 3—Select a region: You will be prompted to choose your region on the following screen. Because it changes the date, time, and other settings on your iPhone, this step is crucial. On this screen, you can swipe up or down to discover your region or hit the search box to find it instantly. After choosing your region, click "Next" to continue.

Step 4—Connect Wi-Fi: You can view a list of Wi-Fi networks that are accessible on the "Wi-Fi" screen. If a Wi-Fi network is available, choose it and type the password when prompted. To finish the setup procedure, if you don't have access to Wi-Fi, you can decide to use your cellular connection. However, to ensure a quicker and more straightforward setup process, we advise using Wi-Fi.

Step 5—Accept Apple's Data & Privacy Terms: After connecting to Wi-Fi, you will be prompted to accept Apple's Data & Privacy Terms. To ensure that you are aware of how Apple collects and utilizes your personal information, you must take this step. Tap "Continue" to continue, then tap "Agree" to concur with the terms and conditions when requested.

Step 6—Installing Face ID: It's now time to activate Face ID, the iPhone 14's face recognition function. By merely gazing at your phone, you may use Face ID to unlock it, make transactions, and access other functions. Hold your phone in front of your face to activate Face ID, then turn your head in a circle as directed by the on-screen prompts. To finish the configuration, you will need to repeat this procedure several times.

Now that the initial setup process is complete, you are ready to go on to the next step. You must choose whether you want to transfer data from an old phone or set up your iPhone as new before moving on.

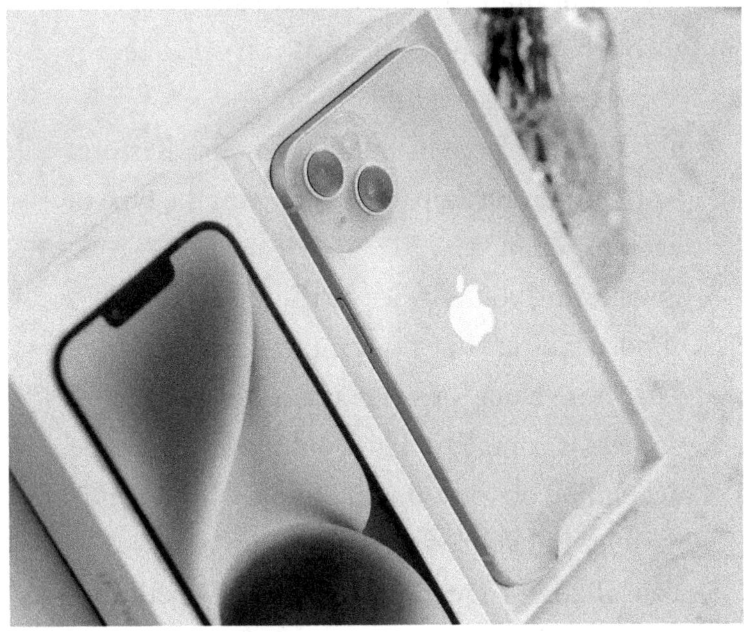

You can transfer data from an outdated iPhone or Android smartphone to your brand-new iPhone 14. For this, Apple has a number of choices, such as recovering from an iCloud or iTunes backup, transferring data directly from an old iPhone, or transferring data from an Android device. The actions for each choice are as follows:

Restoring from an iCloud or iTunes Backup

You can restore data from your old smartphone to your new iPhone 14 if you have an iCloud or iTunes backup of it. Apply the following steps:

1. Start your brand-new iPhone 14 and go through the initial setup until you get to the "Apps & Data" screen.
2. Tap "Restore from iCloud Backup" or "Restore from iTunes Backup," depending on the type of backup you have.
3. By entering your iTunes or iCloud account, choose the backup you want to restore.
4. Keep an eye out for when the restoration process is complete. This could take some time, depending on the amount of your backup and the speed of your Wi-Fi connection.
5. Your iPhone 14 will restart after the restoration process is finished, and you can then continue configuring your device.

Transferring data directly from a previous iPhone

If you already own an iPhone, you can use the Quick Start function on your new iPhone to transfer your data immediately by applying the following steps:

1. Switch on your brand-new iPhone 14 and set it next to your previous model.
2. Select your language and location after setting up Face ID or Touch ID on your new iPhone 14 by following the on-screen prompts.
3. When requested to use your Apple ID to register your new device, tap "Continue" on your old iPhone.
4. To align the animation in the viewfinder, place your old iPhone in front of the new iPhone 14.
5. To start the transfer procedure, enter the passcode for your old iPhone on your new iPhone.
6. Hold off until the transfer is finished. Depending on the volume of information you have, this can take some time.
7. Your iPhone will restart after the transfer is finished, and you can then continue configuring your device.

Moving data from an Android device

If you're transferring data from an Android handset to an iPhone, use the "Move to iOS" app and apply the following steps:

1. On your Android device, download the "Move to iOS" app from the Google Play Store.
2. Switch on your brand-new iPhone 14 and finish the initial setup until you get to the "Apps & Data" screen.
3. On your iPhone 14, click "Move Data from Android" and then choose your Wi-Fi network.
4. On your Android device, launch the "Move to iOS" app and select "Continue."
5. On the "Find Your Code" screen, hit "Agree" to accept the terms and conditions, then tap "Next" in the top-right corner.
6. Tap "Continue" on your iPhone 14 and watch for a code to emerge.
7. After entering the code, wait for the Transfer Data page to display on your Android device.
8. After choosing the data to transfer, touch "Next."
9. Hold off until the transfer is finished. Depending on the volume of information you have, this can take some time.

10. Your iPhone 14 will restart after the transfer is finished, and you can then continue configuring your device.

It is simple and easy to transfer data from your old phone to your new iPhone.

You won't be able to transfer any data from another device to your iPhone if you choose to set it up as a new device. We'll walk you through each step of the procedure in this guide to assist you in setting up your new iPhone.

Step 1: Turn on your iPhone. Start by pushing and holding the power button on the right side of your iPhone to turn it on. The "Hello" screen should first appear on the screen before the Apple logo.

Step 2: Choose your language and region. Swipe left or right on the "Hello" screen until you find your desired language, then tap it to choose it. You will then be asked to select your region. Your area can be found by swiping up or down; tap it to select it.

Step 3: Establish a Wi-Fi connection. You must join a Wi-Fi network in order to proceed with configuring your iPhone. Choose the network you wish to connect to on the Wi-Fi screen, type the password if necessary, and then touch "Join" to join the network.

Step 4: Turn on or off location services. You'll be prompted to allow Location Services after that. This crucial setting gives apps access to your location information. You have the option to allow it right away, later, or completely if you'd rather. Remember that some applications require Location Services to function properly.

Step 5: Setup Touch ID or Face ID. Advanced security features on your iPhone 14 let you securely make purchases and unlock your device, like Face ID or Touch ID. Follow the on-screen prompts to register your face or fingerprint for Face ID or Touch ID setup.

Step 6: Create a passcode. For increased protection, you should always use a passcode on your iPhone. Make a passcode of six digits that is simple for you to remember. Be sure to store this passcode somewhere safe and secure.

Step 7: Setup Siri. Apple's voice-activated personal assistant, Siri, is able to assist you with a variety of activities. Simply follow the on-screen directions to configure Siri and teach it to recognize your voice.

Step 8: Log in using your Apple ID. You must sign in with an Apple ID in order to enjoy your iPhone to its maximum potential. You can sign in right away if you already have an Apple ID. You can create an Apple ID if you don't already have one by clicking "Don't have an Apple ID or forgot it?" on the sign-in screen, then following the on-screen directions to do so.

Step 9: Accept the terms and conditions of Apple. You must consent to Apple's terms and conditions before you may use your iPhone. Tap "Agree" to continue after carefully reading the terms and conditions.

Step 10: Setup iCloud. You can safely save your photographs, movies, documents, and other vital data in the cloud using iCloud, Apple's cloud storage service. Follow the on-screen prompts to sign in with your Apple ID, then select the data you want to sync with iCloud to complete the iCloud setup process.

You've successfully configured your iPhone as a brand-new device. You may immediately begin installing apps, taking pictures, and placing calls. Refer to the previous section on how to transfer data from an old iPhone or Android smartphone if you ever need to transfer data from a previous device.

Notes on SIM Cards and eSIM

This section will be your resource for information about iPhone SIM cards and eSIM. As you may already be aware, your device's SIM card and electronic SIM are necessary for connecting to a cellular network. In this tutorial, we'll give you a quick rundown of SIM cards and eSIMs, along with instructions on how to install and activate them on your iPhone.

What are SIM cards and eSIMs, and what do they do?

You must insert a Subscriber Identity Module (SIM) card into your iPhone 14 in order to connect to your carrier's cellular network. Among the subscriber information that is stored on file are your phone number, contacts, and text messages. In accordance with the needs of the device, SIM cards are available in a variety of sizes, including mini-SIM, micro-SIM, and nano-SIM.

An embedded SIM (eSIM), on the other hand, is an electronic SIM card that is integrated into your iPhone 14. The SIM card is software-based; therefore, there is no need for a physical card because it can be programmed remotely. Because you may activate a new cellular plan on your smartphone without having to go to a carrier store to receive a new physical SIM card, eSIMs are beneficial if you travel regularly or transfer carriers frequently.

How to Insert or Remove SIM Cards from an iPhone

The method of inserting a physical SIM card into your iPhone 14 is simple. This is how you do it:

1. The iPhone's SIM card tray can be found here. In most cases, it can be found on the top of earlier iPhone models or on the right side of the smartphone.
2. Use the SIM ejector tool that came with your iPhone 14 to remove the SIM card tray. You can use a paper clip or a small pin if you don't have the tool.
3. Carefully remove the device's SIM card tray.
4. Place the SIM card in the tray with the notched corner facing the tray's corner and the metal contacts facing downward.
5. Reinstall the SIM card tray by simply pushing it in until it clicks into position.

The procedure for changing SIM cards on your iPhone 14 is comparable. Stick to the same procedures as before, but instead of adding a new SIM card, take out the old one and put in the new one.

Setting up an eSIM on an iPhone 14

Whether your iPhone 14 was bought directly from your carrier or not affects whether you can activate an eSIM on it. Here are the guidelines for both situations:

Setting up an eSIM on an iPhone 14 That Was Bought Directly from Your Carrier:

1. On your iPhone, select Cellular in the Settings app.
2. The Add Cellular Plan option.
3. Follow the instructions displayed on the screen to activate your eSIM.

If you did not purchase your iPhone 14 directly from your carrier, you must activate your eSIM:

1. Get in touch with your carrier and provide them with the QR code for your eSIM, which you can find on your device's box or by getting in touch with your carrier.
2. You will receive additional instructions on how to activate your eSIM from your carrier.

After completing the device setup, activate your eSIM on your iPhone:

1. Select Cellular in the Settings app on your iPhone 14 first.
2. Click on Add Cellular Plan.
3. To activate your eSIM, scan the QR code issued by your carrier.
4. Follow the on-screen instructions to complete the activation procedure.

SIM cards and eSIMs are necessary for your iPhone to be able to connect to your carrier's cellular network. Physical SIM card installation and switching are simple tasks that can be completed quickly. Meanwhile, whether your device was bought directly affects whether it can be activated with an eSIM.

Connecting to Wi-Fi Networks

Utilizing your iPhone requires connecting to Wi-Fi networks. It not only offers a faster and more reliable connection to the internet than cellular data, but it can also lower the cost of your monthly data plan.

You will find detailed instructions on connecting to Wi-Fi networks on your iPhone in this manual:

1. Launch the iPhone's Settings app.
2. Select "Wi-Fi" from the menu of choices.
3. Toggle the switch to turn on Wi-Fi if it is currently off.
4. Your iPhone will start scanning for Wi-Fi networks that are accessible. As soon as one is found, the network's name will be listed under "Choose a Network."
5. Click the network name you want to connect to. You will be asked to enter the password if the network is safe. Correctly enter the password, then select "Join."
6. Your iPhone will join the Wi-Fi network if the password is accurate. The network name will have a checkmark next to it, and the status bar at the top of your iPhone's screen will display the Wi-Fi sign.
7. An error notice noting that the password is incorrect will be shown if it is entered incorrectly. Double-check the password and give it another try.
8. You can manually add the Wi-Fi network if it is not already there by selecting "Other" under "Choose a Network." The network name and

security level should be entered, followed by the password and "Join."

9. Toggle the "Auto-Join" switch to the "on" position if you want your iPhone to automatically connect to this Wi-Fi network whenever it is within range.

10. Try shutting off and then turning back on Wi-Fi on your iPhone if you're having problems connecting to a Wi-Fi network. Restarting your iPhone and clearing its network settings are further options.

Keep in mind that since public Wi-Fi networks are frequently unprotected, joining one can be dangerous. Avoid entering important information, such as passwords or credit card numbers, while using public Wi-Fi in order to stay safe. Only connect to trusted networks.

CUSTOMIZING YOUR WALLPAPER, SOUNDS, AND VIBRATION SETTINGS

How to Change Your iPhone's Wallpaper

Changing the background and ringtones on your iPhone is one of the simplest ways to start customizing it. We'll outline easy instructions for changing your iPhone's wallpaper in this post.

Step 1: Launch the settings program. On your home screen, find the "Settings" app first. It resembles the gear icon. To open it, tap on it.

Step 2: Select "Wallpaper." Go to the "Settings" app and scroll down until you find "Wallpaper." To access the wallpaper settings, tap on them.

Step 3: Choose a new wallpaper. You can select from a number of alternatives under the "Wallpaper" settings, including "Choose a New Wallpaper," "Dynamic," "Stills," or "Live." To choose from the pre-loaded wallpaper options or to browse through your photos, tap "Choose a New Wallpaper" on the wallpaper menu.

Step 4: Set the wallpaper. You can set a wallpaper as your lock screen, home screen, or both after choosing one. By zooming in or out and dragging the image to the desired spot, you can easily make adjustments to the image. When you're satisfied with your choice, touch "Set" to make the modifications.

Step 5: Customize sounds. Additionally, you can modify the sounds on your iPhone 14 via the "Settings" app. To access the sound options, tap "Sounds" in the same "Wallpaper" settings. You can then edit the vibrations, text tones, and ringtones.

Making your iPhone feel more unique is simple and enjoyable by changing the wallpaper and audio. It's crucial to remember that the procedure could change significantly based on the software and version of your iPhone. To fully customize your iPhone 14 experience, it's always a good idea to check out all of the settings and choices you have in the "Settings" app.

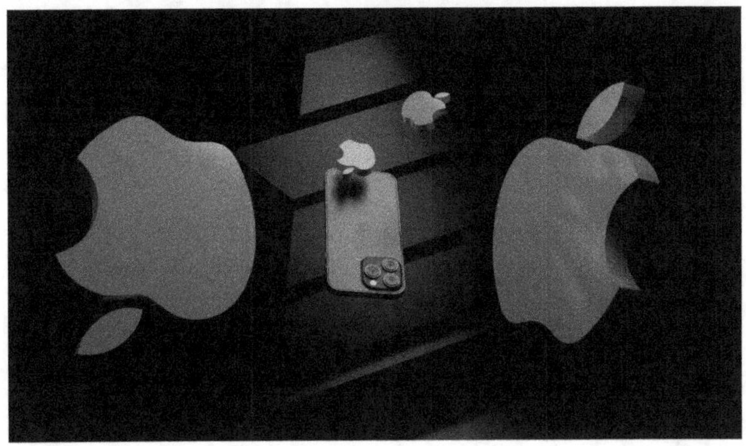

Customizing Sounds on Your iPhone

Along with the instructions for the other sound types, below are the methods for customizing the "Timer Tone" and "Keyboard Sound" on your iPhone 14:

Ringtone

1. Start your iPhone 14's Settings application.
2. Click "Sounds & Haptics."
3. Click "Ringtone."
4. Choose a different tone.

5. A tone preview.
6. Set the tone to default.
7. Save your changes.

Text Tone

1. Get your iPhone's Settings app open.
2. Click or tap "Sounds & Haptics."
3. Click or tap "Text Tone."
4. Change your tone.
5. Examine the tone.
6. Decide on a default tone.
7. Save your edits.

Other Tone

1. Get your iPhone's Settings app open.
2. Click or tap "Sounds & Haptics."
3. Click or tap "Other Tone."
4. Change your tone.
5. Examine the tone.
6. Decide on a default tone.
7. Save your changes.

Alarm Tone

1. Open the Clock app on your iPhone 14.
2. Tap on "Edit" in the top left corner of the screen.
3. Tap on the alarm you want to customize.
4. Tap on "Sound."
5. Choose a new tone.
6. Preview the tone.
7. Set the tone as your default.
8. Save your changes.

Timer Tone

1. Open the Clock app on your iPhone 14.
2. Tap on "Timer."
3. Tap on "When Timer Ends."
4. Change your tone.
5. Examine the tone.
6. Decide on a default tone.
7. Save your edits.

Keyboard Sound

1. Open the Settings app on your iPhone 14.
2. Tap on "Sounds & Haptics."
3. Scroll down to "Keyboard Clicks."

4. Turn on the toggle switch if it is not already on.
5. Try out the different options to choose a keyboard sound that you like.

It's simple to customize the various sound types on your iPhone by choosing a new tone, previewing it, setting it as your default, and saving your modifications. You can customize your smartphone and make it more fun to use by following these instructions.

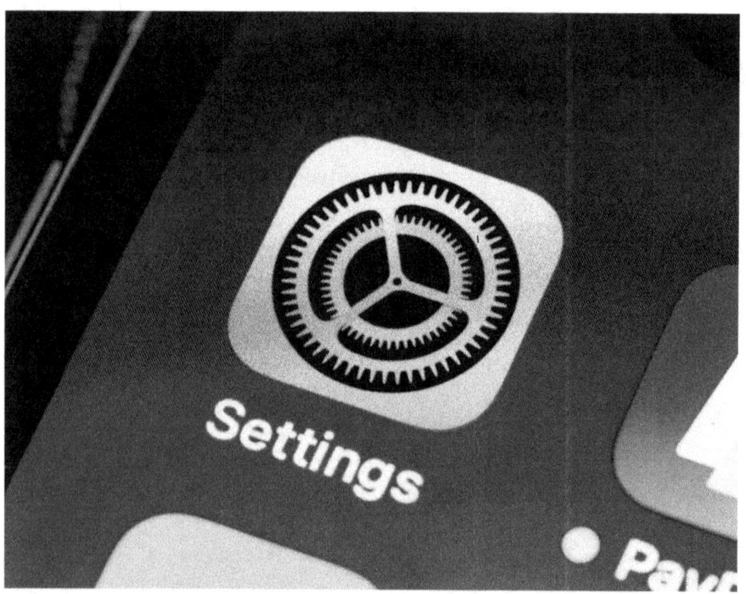

Setting Vibrations

You can quickly set up vibrations on your iPhone 14 by following these easy instructions if you prefer that incoming calls and notifications vibrate instead of sound:

1. Launch Settings. Locate and press the "Settings" app, which is denoted by a gear icon, on your iPhone's home screen.
2. Open the Sounds & Haptics menu. Click "Sounds & Haptics" after scrolling down. The Sounds & Haptics settings page will then be displayed.
3. Select vibration choices. The "Vibrate" section of the Sounds & Haptics page offers a choice of vibration settings. Tap on "Ringtone" or "Text Tone" to choose the desired vibration pattern.
4. Check for vibrations. You can test the vibration pattern you choose by tapping on the "Vibration" option at the top of the screen and then tapping on the pattern you want to use.

Setting a Customized Vibration Alert on the iPhone

You can modify vibration alerts on your iPhone by following these instructions if you want to make a special vibration pattern for a certain contact or app or disable vibrations for particular notifications:

1. Open Settings or Contacts. Open either the Contacts app or the Settings app, depending on

whether you want to personalize vibration alerts for a specific contact or for all apps.

2. Pick a contact or an application. Select the contact from your Contacts app if you are personalizing vibration alerts for a particular contact. If you wish to personalize an all-purpose app, go to "Settings" and choose the desired app.

3. Select options for vibration. To access the vibration options for a contact, touch "Edit" and then "Ringtone" or "Text Tone." To access the vibration options for an app, go down and touch on "Sounds & Haptics."

4. Create a custom vibration pattern. Once you've selected a vibration option, scroll down to the "Custom" section and tap on "Create New Vibration." Tap on the screen to create a custom vibration pattern, and then tap "Stop" when you're finished.

5. Assign the custom vibration pattern. Give your custom vibration pattern a name, and then tap "Save" to assign it to the selected contact or app.

By following these steps, you can set up both standard and customized vibration alerts on your iPhone 14, giving you greater control over your device's notifications.

SETTING UP AND CUSTOMIZING YOUR CONTROL CENTER FOR QUICK ACCESS TO KEY FEATURES

Apple devices have a feature called Control Center that enables users to easily access and manage certain settings and features without navigating through menus or settings. Since iOS 7's first release, it has evolved into a common feature on iPhones, iPads, and iPod touch.

To access the Control Center on an iPhone 14, scroll down from the top-right corner of the screen. Quick access to frequently used functions, including Wi-Fi, Bluetooth, Airplane mode, Do Not Disturb, and screen brightness, is provided by the Control Center. Additionally, it has options for the camera settings, screen recording, and music playback.

Control Center's ability to be customized to include extra functions and shortcuts is one of its most helpful features. It can be customized and made to be an effective tool by the users, who can add or remove controls based on their needs and preferences. Users may include controls for devices like the flashlight, calculator, and even Apple TV.

Control Center is useful, but it also saves battery life by making it simple for users to disable features when not in use. For instance, conserving battery life can be achieved by turning off Bluetooth or Wi-Fi when not required.

How to access the Access Control Center

On your iPhone, Control Center is a strong utility that gives you rapid access to key settings and capabilities. Control Center makes it simple to perform a variety of tasks without having to go through a number of menus, like turning on or off Wi-Fi, Bluetooth, Airplane Mode, adjusting screen brightness or volume, and managing media playback.

On the iPhone, swipe down from the top-right corner of the screen to reach the Control Center. The swipe-down gesture, however, can only be used if you begin from the top-right corner of the screen, as this is where the Control Center icon is situated.

On more current iPhone models, such as the iPhone 14, you can also access the Control Center from the lock screen by swiping down from the top-right corner of the screen. If you need to rapidly access a setting or feature when your phone is locked, this can be really helpful.

When you first open the Control Center, you'll notice a variety of icons that stand in for various settings and functionality. Simply tap on the corresponding symbol to access any of these options or functions. For instance, to change the screen brightness, simply tap the brightness slider and set the appropriate amount.

The Control Center can also be customized by adding or removing icons. To do this, open Settings, choose Control Center, and then choose Customize Controls. By tapping the green plus or red minus icons next to each choice, you can add or remove icons from this point.

You can add shortcuts to outside applications in addition to personalizing the Control Center's iconography. For instance, you can create a shortcut to an app that you commonly use in the Control Center for quick and simple access.

How to Use Control Center

The iPhone's Control Center provides easy access to a number of settings and functionality. Here are several methods for enhancing your iPhone experience with Control Center:

- Volume: From the Control Center, you may change the volume of your iPhone's ringer, notifications, and media playing. Simply swipe up from the bottom of the screen to launch the

Control Center, then use the slider to adjust the volume.

- Brightness: From the Control Center, you may also change the brightness of your screen if necessary. Swipe up from the bottom of the screen to reopen the Control Center. Then, using the brightness slider, change the brightness to your preference.

- Music: Through the Control Center, you can now manage the volume and playback controls for music on your iPhone. You don't need to launch the Music app to pause, skip tracks, or change the volume when listening to music on your iPhone by using the Control Center.

- Focus mode: One of the most recent additions to iOS 15 is Focus mode, which enables you to choose personalized distraction-reduction settings and customize your iPhone experience to suit your current task. By touching the Focus button in Control Center, you can immediately enter Focus mode.

- Screen mirroring: If necessary, you can use the Control Center to mirror the iPhone's screen to a different screen or device. Select the device you wish to link to by first tapping the Screen Mirroring button in the Control Center.

- Rotation lock: From Control Center, you may choose to preserve your iPhone's screen orientation in either portrait or landscape mode. To enable or disable the rotation lock, tap the Rotation Lock button.

These are only a few methods for quickly gaining access to key settings and functionality on your iPhone by using Control Center. Keep in mind that the Control Center can be customized to add or delete buttons and features that you commonly use. To do this, navigate to Settings > Control Center > Customize Controls.

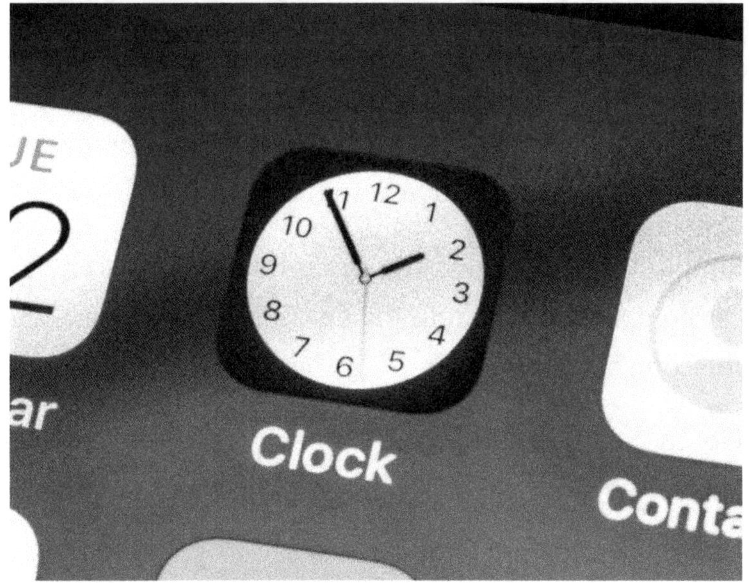

How to Customize Control Center to Include the Features You Use Most Frequently

You can modify the Control Center on your iPhone to include the features you use the most often in order to get the most out of it. You will be able to access those functions more quickly and easily thanks to this.

You can add or delete controls, reorder them, or disable Control Center entirely to make it your own. You can select the functions you wish to see in the Control Center by adding or removing controls, and you can prioritize the most crucial functionality by rearranging the controls.

Go to Settings > Control Center > Customize Controls to add or remove controls. You can add or delete controls from this list by tapping the plus or minus buttons that are located next to them.

Simply touch and hold the three-line icon adjacent to the control and drag it to the new location to rearrange the controls.

Go to Settings > Control Center and deactivate the "Access Within Apps" setting if you want to disable Control Center.

This chapter helps you personalize your iPhone and make it your own, emphasizing that it's more than just a device. It begins by providing a comprehensive guide to the basic setup procedure, including tips on personalizing your iPhone's wallpaper, audio, vibration, and control center. With these suggestions, you can be more effective and productive while also feeling more in control and at ease using your smartphone. In the next chapter, we'll delve into communication on your iPhone, including calls, messages, and emails. Stay tuned for expert advice on maximizing your communication experience on your iPhone.

2

CONNECTING WITH LOVED ONES

Your iPhone serves as a multifunctional communication hub in addition to being a phone. It has a number of built-in functions and apps that make it simple to interact with your loved ones. In this chapter, we'll look at how to use your iPhone to stay in touch with your loved ones wherever you go.

Your iPhone is a flexible tool for staying connected, allowing you to do everything from place calls and send texts to use social media apps and video chat. We also looked into the tools and apps that can facilitate communication, like Siri, dictation, and Do Not Disturb mode. With your iPhone in hand, stay in touch with your loved ones wherever you go.

MAKING AND RECEIVING CALLS WITH EASE USING THE PHONE APP

Your iPhone's Phone app is a crucial component that enables audio calls between you and your loved ones, family, and coworkers. Here are a few of the Phone app's fundamental attributes:

Calling instructions: Simply launch the Phone app on your iPhone and tap the "Keypad" icon at the bottom of the screen to place a call. Enter the required phone number after that, then click the green "Call" button. By selecting the person you wish to call by tapping on the "Contacts" icon, you can also call someone from your contacts list as an alternative.

Calling contacts: You can call people on your contacts list using the Phone app. Open the Phone app, then tap the "Contacts" icon to accomplish this. Next, touch on the person's phone number after choosing who you wish to call. Automatically, the call will begin.

Favorite contacts list creation: You can create a list of your favorite contacts using the Phone app. To do this, launch the Phone app and choose the "Favorites" icon. Next, click the "+" button to add a contact to your list of favorites. Once a contact is added, you can call them right away by touching on their name in the Favorites list.

Answering and rejecting calls: When someone calls, your iPhone will ring, and a notification will show up on your screen. Swipe the green "Answer" button to answer the call. Swipe the red "Decline" button if you don't want to answer the phone. By tapping the "Message" icon, you can reject a call and leave a message for the caller.

Using applications during calls: Some iPhone apps, such as Notes, Messages, and FaceTime, can be used while on a call. Simply hit the "Home" button to get back to your home screen and launch the desired app. You can move between the app and the call as necessary while the call is still being made in the background.

Voicemail: You may access your voicemail using the Phone app as well. To do this, open the Phone app and tap the "Voicemail" icon. Your voicemail messages are available for listening and can be saved or deleted as needed. There will be a notification on your screen if you have a new voicemail. By selecting the "Greeting" option under Voicemail Settings, you can also create a personalized voicemail greeting.

USING FACETIME FOR VIDEO CALLS

Apple created the video and audio calling software FaceTime. You can make free video and audio calls to other Apple users as long as you have access to Wi-Fi or cellular data. FaceTime calls can be made on an iPhone, iPad, or Mac computer.

The difference between FaceTime calls and ordinary phone calls is that FaceTime calls need an internet connection. Contrarily, phone calls utilize a cellular network. Another significant distinction is that FaceTime supports visual calls, whereas traditional phone calls only support audio. Additionally, unlike ordinary phone calls, which can be placed to anybody with a phone number, FaceTime calls can only be placed to other Apple users who also have the FaceTime software.

FaceTime has the benefit of allowing you to see the person you are speaking to, which makes for a more personal and interesting exchange. Additionally, as long as you have an internet connection, FaceTime calls are free, which might help you save money on your phone bill.

FaceTime calls do use data, but they are not included in your cellular plan's data consumption, which is crucial to note. FaceTime can quickly consume a lot of bandwidth, so if you're using it on a cellular network and don't have unlimited data, you should be aware of this.

For communicating with friends, family, and coworkers, FaceTime is generally a practical and convenient tool. FaceTime may make communicating with others more personal and private, whether you're using it for a brief catch-up chat or a business conference.

FaceTime on the iPhone 14 is straightforward to set up and only requires a few quick steps. How to set up FaceTime is as follows:

1. Start your iPhone 14's Settings application.
2. Choose FaceTime by scrolling down the page.
3. To activate FaceTime, turn the switch next to it on.
4. When prompted, enter your Apple ID and password. You'll skip this step if you're already logged in.
5. Select the contact details you want to use for FaceTime, including email addresses. As necessary, you can add or remove addresses.

There you have it! FaceTime is now set up on your iPhone 14.

To make a FaceTime call, use the Phone app or the Contacts app. Simply choose the person you wish to call in the Contacts app and touch the FaceTime icon.

Using the Phone app, select the contact, then hit the FaceTime icon.

Keep in mind that if you place a FaceTime call to a person who does not own an iPhone or iPad, FaceTime will not be available. But you may still use FaceTime Audio to call them on an audio-only basis.

Once you've made sure you have an internet connection, take these actions to place a FaceTime call:

1. Open FaceTime on your iPhone 14 in the first place. It has a white video camera and a green symbol.
2. Click or tap the plus sign (+) in the top-right corner of the screen.
3. Type the person's name, contact information, or email address. You can tap on a name to pick a contact if they are already in your contact list.
4. Tap the video or audio option to select a FaceTime call with video or audio.
5. You might need to choose the correct phone number or email address if your contact has more than one.
6. Press the green phone or video button to place the call.

7. Hold off until the other party answers your phone. Leave a FaceTime voicemail if the person isn't available.

Whether you are nearby or far away, placing a FaceTime call on your iPhone 14 is often a quick and simple way to communicate with loved ones. You can easily begin a video or voice call with someone in your contacts list by entering their phone number or email address or by using the steps listed above.

It's easy to respond to a FaceTime audio call on an iPhone 14. Your iPhone will ring when you get a FaceTime audio call, and the screen will show the caller's name and picture. Swipe up to the FaceTime icon from the green phone icon to answer the call. Tap the "Accept" button to begin the call.

A fantastic way to ask somebody to join a call is by creating a FaceTime call link. Open the FaceTime app on your iPhone 14 and start a new call to make a FaceTime call. Touch the "i" icon next to the person's name after choosing who you wish to call, then touch "Create Link." You can send a new link to other people via text message, email, or any other messaging service.

When someone taps the link, the FaceTime software on their iPhone or iPad will launch, and they will be added to the call automatically. If you want to invite someone who isn't on your contact list or for group calls, this is a helpful alternative.

Basically, you can answer a FaceTime audio call on your iPhone 14 by swiping up from the green phone symbol, and you can make a FaceTime call link by starting a new call, clicking the "i" button, and choosing "Create Link."

A great way to explain something on your iPhone, iPad, or Mac to someone is by using FaceTime to share your screen. Fortunately, sharing your screen during a FaceTime chat is simple. Here's how to go about it:

- Make a FaceTime call to the other person before sharing your screen. Once you are on the call, you must activate the screen-sharing feature.
- To share your screen on an iPhone or iPad, swipe up from the bottom of the screen to expose the Control Center, then press the Screen Mirroring icon. After selecting your Apple TV, iPad, or Mac from the list of eligible devices, turn on Mirroring.
- You can share your screen during a FaceTime conversation on a Mac by clicking the Share Screen icon. You can choose to share only a specific program window or your entire screen.

Once you've made your decision, select the Share option to show the other person your screen.

- Make sure to close any personal or sensitive information on your screen before sharing it during a FaceTime chat because the person on the other end will be able to see everything on your screen, including alerts.

A fantastic way to contribute and aid someone in understanding something on your smartphone during a FaceTime chat is to share your screen. You can quickly share your screen and make your point with only a few simple actions.

If you have an iPhone 14, you can filter background noise during a FaceTime conversation in a number of ways. One choice is to blur the background; this might assist in keeping the attention on you and away from your surroundings. Simply launch the FaceTime app, touch on the three dots in the top-right corner, and choose "Blur my background" to accomplish this.

Activating Live Captions, which will caption everything stated throughout the session, is an additional choice. For those who have hearing loss or are in noisy situations, this can be especially useful. Navigate to Settings, choose Accessibility, and then Live Caption to enable live captioning. The next time you use FaceTime, Live Captions will be available if you flip the switch to the on position.

Regardless of your circumstances or hearing abilities, these features can help you make your FaceTime calls more efficient and pleasurable. You can modify your call settings and block distracting background noise with only a few taps.

STAYING IN TOUCH WITH MESSAGES

Both iMessage and standard SMS can be used to send text messages on an iPhone. iMessage is Apple's instant messaging service that enables you to communicate with other iPhone, iPad, or Mac users online while sending text, images, videos, and other sorts of media. Regular SMS is a common text messaging service that works with any smartphone and sends messages via your cellular network.

To enable iMessage, navigate to "Settings" > "Messages" and slide the iMessage switch to the on position. When iMessage is turned on, it will be automatically used when sending messages to other iPhone, iPad, or Mac users, and the discussion bubbles will be blue rather than green.

You can also set or disable read receipts, which inform the sender when their message has been read by the receiver. Go to "Settings" > "Messages" > "Send Read Receipts" and flip the button to enable or disable read receipts.

By adding your name and photo, you can further personalize your iMessage account. To achieve this, navigate to "Settings" > "Messages" > "Share Name and Photo" and pick your desired profile photo.

It is simple to add files and media to messages. To capture a photograph or a video, tap the camera icon. To upload a picture, a video, or a file, tap the App Store icon. The microphone icon can also be used to record and deliver audio messages.

You can instantly undo a message you unintentionally sent or a mistake you made by shaking your phone and choosing "Undo." Another way to alter a message that has already been sent is to double-tap on the message bubble and choose "Edit" or "Delete."

It's practical to reply from the lock screen when you need to answer a message right away. On the notice, just swipe left and select "Reply."

By "pinning" them, you can keep your most important interactions at the top of your Messages list. Swipe right on the discussion and hit the pin symbol to save it.

Sending a group message involves opening a new message and including a number of recipients in order to start a group conversation. By hitting the "i" button in the conversation's upper right corner, choosing "Add Contact," and then choosing the person you wish to add, you may easily include more people in an already-existing group chat. A group discussion can be left by tapping the "i" icon, scrolling down, and choosing "Leave this Conversation."

MANAGING YOUR CONTACTS

The iPhone's Contacts app is a crucial component that enables you to save, manage, and quickly access the contact information of your friends, family, and coworkers. Here's how to configure it:

1. First, launch the Contacts app: The Contacts app icon, which resembles an address book, is typically found on the iPhone home screen. To launch the app, tap the icon.
2. Permit access to your contacts: When you open the Contacts app for the first time, your iPhone will ask for access to your contacts. To allow access, tap "Allow."
3. Add a Contact: Tap the "+" icon in the top-right corner of the screen to add a new contact. The

contact's name, phone number, email address, and additional information, like their address, website, and notes, can then be entered.

4. Edit an Existing Contact: To view a contact's information, tap on their name. Then click "Edit" in the top-right corner of the screen. Then, you can change their name, phone number, email address, and other details associated with their contact information.

5. Sync your contacts: If you use several devices, such as an iPad or a MacBook, you may sync your contacts to keep them current on all of them. To activate the Contacts toggle, navigate to Settings > iCloud on your iPhone.

6. Group your Contacts: You may also divide your contacts into lists like friends, family, and coworkers. To do this, select the lists you wish to display by tapping "lists" in the top left corner of the Contacts app.

7. Find a Contact: Finding a specific contact can be difficult if you have a large number of contacts. On the other hand, you may quickly discover the contact you're looking for by utilizing the search bar at the top of the Contacts app.

To sum up, the iPhone's Contacts app is a strong tool for maintaining your contacts. You can quickly set up, edit, and organize your contacts by following these steps, ensuring that you always have access to their information when you need it. Keep it in mind to sync your contacts and group them for quick access.

With these useful hints, managing your contacts on the iPhone 14 can be a breeze. Let's look at how to add and remove contacts, sort and modify your contacts, add and remove favorites, block contacts, share contacts, and start a conversation via the Contacts app.

Organizing by first or last name, adding images, and establishing groups are all ways to personalize and organize your contacts on the iPhone. To create a group, open the Contacts app and select "Lists." Tap "Create New List" after that, then give your list a name. By selecting the contacts you want to add and hitting "Edit" in the top-right corner of the screen, you can then add contacts to the list. Tap "Edit" after selecting a contact's name to add a photo. To choose a photo from your camera roll or take a new one, tap on their photo and choose "Choose Photo." You may also choose to sort your contacts by first or last name by navigating to "Settings," "Contacts," and then "Sort Order."

Adding New Contacts: Open the Contacts app on your iPhone 14 and hit the "+" icon in the top-right corner of the screen to add a new contact. Enter the contact's name, phone number, email address, and any other relevant information. When finished, simply tap "Done" to save the new contact to your phone.

Deleting Contacts: On your iPhone, open the Contacts app and search for the contact you want to delete. Then, in the top-right corner of the screen, tap "Edit" after tapping on their name. In the bottom section, scroll down and select "Delete Contact." Once you confirm you want to delete the contact, it will be taken off your phone.

Making a Contact a Favorite: Open the Contacts app on your iPhone and look for the person you want to make a favorite. After tapping on their name, select the star button next to it. The person will now be included in your list of Favorites.

Removal of a Favorite Contact: Open the Contacts app on your iPhone and select "Favorites" to get rid of a favorite contact. To remove a contact, swipe left on their name and click "Remove."

Contact Blocking: Search for the person you want to block in the Contacts app on your iPhone. Following your tap on their name, scroll to the bottom and choose "Block this Caller." When you choose to block a contact, they won't be able to call or text you again.

Contact sharing: Open the Contacts app on your iPhone and look for the contact you wish to share. After tapping on their name, select "Share Contact." The method you want to use to distribute the contact, such as text message or email, is then your choice.

Choosing a Communication Mode in the Contacts App: You can choose a communication mode, such as phoning, texting, or emailing, by tapping on the contact you wish to contact in the Contacts app on your iPhone. Additionally, you can start a conversation simply by tapping down on a contact's name in the Contacts app to access the "Quick Actions" option.

Customizing and arranging your contacts, adding and deleting contacts, marking a contact as a favorite, removing a favorite contact, blocking contacts, sharing contacts, and starting conversations from the Contacts app may make managing your contacts on the iPhone 14 a seamless experience. To maintain your organization and relationships with your contacts, follow these procedures.

CHECKING EMAIL ON YOUR IPHONE

Using email on your iPhone 14 can be incredibly convenient. Email is a vital communication tool. On your iPhone, follow these exact instructions to add email accounts, deactivate email accounts, and send emails with attachments.

Your iPhone can easily and automatically add an email account. On the official Apple support page, follow these instructions to set up your email account automatically:

1. Select Add Account under Settings > Passwords & Accounts.
2. Decide on an email provider.
3. After entering your email address and password, proceed as directed on the screen.

If automatic setup is not an option for you, you can still set up your email account manually. You must be aware of the settings for your email account, including your email address, incoming mail server, and outgoing mail server.

Follow these procedures to remove an email account from your iPhone:

1. Firstly, navigate to Settings > Passwords & Accounts.
2. Tap the email account you wish to unsubscribe from.

3. Select Delete Account, then verify that you wish to do so.

On the iPhone, sending emails and including attachments is also simple. Open the Mail app on your iPhone first, then perform the following actions:

1. Click the Compose button (the pencil and paper-shaped icon).
2. Fill out the "To" field with the recipient's email address.
3. Fill up the "Subject" field with a subject for your email.
4. Fill out the email's body with your message.
5. Tap and hold the email's body until a menu opens to add an attachment. By tapping the arrow on the right side of the menu, choose Add Attachment.
6. From the files on your iPhone, select the file you wish to attach, then tap Add.

You are now prepared to submit your email.

UNDERSTANDING AND CUSTOMIZING YOUR NOTIFICATION SETTINGS TO STAY ON TOP OF COMMUNICATIONS

Managing Messages notifications: Open the Settings app, choose Notifications, and then choose Messages to manage Messages notifications on your iPhone. From this point, you may select whether or not to receive notifications for new messages, whether to display or conceal message previews, and whether to combine or split notifications by discussion.

Changing message sounds: Go to Settings, select Sounds & Haptics, and then scroll down to the Sounds and Vibration Patterns section to alter the sound for incoming messages. Select a new sound from the list of selections after selecting the "Text Tone" option, or enter your own audio file to create a unique sound.

How to assign sounds to specific contacts: Open the Contacts app, choose the relevant contact, touch on Edit, and then tap on Text Tone to change the sound that will be played when that person sends you a message. You can select an incoming message sound for that contact from this point on.

Conversation notification muting: If you notice that a certain conversation is producing an excessive number of alerts, you can turn off notification generation for that conversation. Toggle the "Hide Alerts" option by going to the Messages app, choosing the relevant discussion, and then tapping the "i" icon in the top-right corner. Until you disable the Hide Alerts function, this will stop notifications for that conversation from showing up on your lock screen or in the notification center.

Do Not Disturb and Focus Mode: Managing notifications on your iPhone can be made easier with the help of these two capabilities. You can choose the alerts you receive in focus mode based on the current activity you are engaged in, such as work or personal time. Go to Settings, click Focus, and then pick the desired Focus option to enable Focus mode. Contrarily, Do Not Disturb enables you to disable notifications for a predetermined duration, such as while you are in a meeting or asleep. By heading to Settings, choosing Do Not Disturb, and then turning it on, you can activate Do Not Disturb.

Hide alerts: You can use Hide Alerts to entirely hide notifications for a certain chat. Toggle the "Hide Alerts" option by going to the Messages app, choosing the relevant discussion, and then tapping the "i" icon in the top-right corner. Until you disable the Hide Alerts function, this will stop notifications for that conversation from showing up on your lock screen or in the notification center.

This chapter shows how to create a favorites list, answer and reject calls, and use different apps while on calls. It also discusses how to use FaceTime, Apple's video and audio calling software, which requires an internet connection and can only be used with other Apple users who have the FaceTime software. The chapter concludes with instructions on how to create a FaceTime call link and how to use FaceTime to share your screen. The next chapter will explain how to access information and the internet on your iPhone.

3

HOW TO ACCESS INFORMATION ANYTIME, ANYWHERE

As the world becomes more digital, having access to the internet is becoming more and more crucial. Fortunately, an iPhone allows you to instantly access the web and all of the information it has to offer. Imagine having access to all available knowledge wherever you go.

In this chapter, we'll look at how to utilize your iPhone to access the internet, do informational searches, and visit websites. We'll also look at some pointers and methods for making the most of your iPhone's online browsing capabilities.

Having an iPhone can be a useful tool for accessing the web and all its knowledge, whether you're a student doing research for a paper, a professional seeking material work, or just someone who enjoys learning new things. So let's get started and see how we can maximize it.

USING SAFARI FOR WEB BROWSING AND ONLINE SEARCHES

The iPhone 14's default web browser is Safari. It enables users to connect with websites, explore the internet, and get information. The following elements of the Safari interface make browsing easier:

1. Smart Search Bar: At the top of the Safari screen is the Smart Search Bar. Users can enter a web address or search phrase using this as both the address bar and the search bar. Safari provides results as users type, making it simple to find what you're looking for.
2. Web navigation: There are a number of ways to move around the web. Simply tap the top of the screen to return to the website's homepage. To get back to the top of the website, just tap the top of the screen. You only need to swipe down from the top edge of the screen to expose the Safari address bar.
3. Using Tabs: Users can open several websites simultaneously using tabs. Tap the "+" symbol

in the top-right corner of the Safari screen to open a new tab. Swipe left or right with two fingers to switch between tabs.

4. Bookmarking Pages: For quick access, users can bookmark frequently visited pages. Tap the "Share" icon at the bottom of the Safari screen and choose "Add Bookmark" to bookmark a page. Tap the "Bookmarks" icon at the bottom of the Safari screen to access your bookmarks.

5. Sharing Links: Sending links to friends, relatives, or coworkers is a fantastic way to share knowledge. Tap the "Share" button at the bottom of the Safari screen to share a link, then choose how you want to share it.

6. Private Browsing: Private Browsing enables users to browse the web anonymously by erasing cookies and browsing histories. Press the "Tabs" icon at the bottom of the Safari screen, then press "Private" to start Private Browsing. Additionally, you can turn on Private Browsing in the Settings application by going to "Safari" > "Private Browsing."

On the iPhone 14, deleting your browsing history is simple and can help preserve your privacy. Safari's web browser records the websites you visit, as well as your search history and other browsing information. This information can help you remember website passwords and complete forms more quickly, but if you're concerned that someone else might access it, you might wish to wipe your history.

Follow these instructions to delete your internet history on your iPhone 14:

1. Launch Safari and select the bookmarks icon (the one that looks like a book open).
2. To view your browser history, tap the clock symbol in the top-left corner.
3. Select "Clear" from the screen's bottom menu.
4. Select the time period for which you wish to erase your browsing history, such as "the last hour," "today," or "all time."
5. To confirm, tap "Clear History."

By navigating to Settings > Safari > Clear History and Website Data, you can delete your cookies and cache in addition to your browsing history. All saved information, such as login credentials and other website preferences, will be deleted as a result.

Your browsing experience on the iPhone 14 can be improved and customized by configuring Safari. Here are several methods for modifying Safari:

1. Text Size: To make the text in Safari easier to read, you can change the size of the font used. Go to any website in Safari and change the text size there. Pinch your fingers together or apart to enlarge or minimize the text on the screen.

2. Display and Privacy Controls: The display and privacy controls in Safari can also be adjusted to your tastes. In order to do this, select "Settings" and then "Safari." From there, you can manage several options, including blocking pop-ups, turning on or off JavaScript, and modifying your privacy and security settings.

Overall, personalizing Safari on your iPhone 14 might make your browsing experience more suited to your requirements and preferences.

ACCESSING ICLOUD

Apple Inc. created the cloud storage and syncing service known as iCloud. You can use any of your Apple devices to view your files and data that are stored remotely. It has a number of features that make managing and storing your data with it simple and effective. To access iCloud, go to iCloud.com in your browser and click search.

The following are some of the standard iCloud features:

iCloud Backup: This function automatically backs up all of the data on your iPhone to iCloud, including your contacts, photos, and videos. In the event that your iPhone is lost or broken, make sure you have a backup of your data.

Find My: You may use this function to find all of your Apple devices that have an active iCloud account, such as your iPhone, iPad, and Mac. To protect your data, you can also remotely lock or erase any stolen or misplaced devices.

iCloud Drive: With this function, you may save your papers and files in iCloud and access them from any Apple device. Additionally, you can collaborate in real-time on documents and share data with others.

iCloud photographs: Using this function, all of your photographs and videos are automatically backed up to iCloud and are accessible from any Apple device. Additionally, you can create albums and share your images with others.

Keychain: This program securely stores your passwords, credit card numbers, and other sensitive information across all of your Apple devices. Additionally, it creates secure passwords for you and automatically fills them in, saving you time and effort.

1. App Sync: With the help of this function, all the data from your apps are synced between all of your Apple devices. It implies that you won't have to restart an app after leaving it on any of your devices.
2. Hide My Email: With the help of this function, you can make one-of-a-kind, arbitrary email addresses that are forward to your actual email address. You can reduce spam in your mailbox and preserve your privacy.

All things considered, iCloud is a flexible and strong solution that can assist you in managing and safeguarding your data across all of your Apple devices.

1. Some of the things your iPhone can do using iCloud include the following:
2. Backup your data to iCloud to protect it in case your smartphone is stolen or ruined.
3. To access your photos and movies on all of your devices, use iCloud Pictures.
4. Use iCloud Contacts and iCloud Calendar to keep your contacts, calendars, and other crucial data synchronized across all of your devices.

5. To store your files and have access to them from anywhere, use iCloud Drive.
6. Use iCloud Drive to collaborate and share files with others.
7. Keep your credit card numbers and passwords up-to-date and synchronized across all of your devices by using iCloud Keychain.
8. Make use of Find My to find a missing device or to find friends and family who have shared their locations with you.
9. To access your email on all of your devices, use iCloud Mail.
10. Use Hide My Email to preserve your privacy and hide your email address from spammers.
11. To quickly and easily configure a new device, use iCloud.

How to configure iCloud on an iPhone

1. First, make sure your iPhone is using the most recent iOS version.
2. Open Settings on your iPhone and select your Apple ID name at the top of the page.
3. After selecting iCloud, enter your Apple ID and password to log in. To create an Apple ID if you don't already have one, click "Get a Free Apple ID" and follow the instructions.

4. Which iCloud functions you want to use will be requested of you. On/off switches for iCloud Backup, iCloud Drive, and iCloud Photos may be found here.
5. Follow the instructions to configure each function, such as choosing which files you want to save in iCloud Drive or which apps you want to back up for iCloud Backup.

Activating iCloud Drive:

1. Open the Settings app on your iPhone and select your Apple ID name at the top of the screen.
2. Tap iCloud, then go down to iCloud Drive.
3. Turn on the iCloud Drive switch.
4. You have the choice to allow or stop the ability to transfer files using cellular data.
5. Another choice is to have your iPhone's Home screen show the iCloud Drive app.

Once enabled, you can access your iCloud Drive using the Files app on your iPhone. From your other Apple devices that are logged into the same Apple ID, you may then view any files that you have saved in iCloud Drive.

USING THE APP STORE TO FIND AND DOWNLOAD APPS THAT MEET YOUR NEEDS

Applications are collections of software programs created especially for mobile devices like smartphones and tablets. These apps can be found and downloaded via the App Store, a platform for finding and downloading mobile apps that are compatible with iOS devices for a variety of uses, including productivity, entertainment, education, and communication.

The App Store offers a variety of popular mobile app categories, including:

1. Educational applications: These apps are made to offer users knowledge and learning possibilities in a variety of subjects, including history, arithmetic, science, and language acquisition.
2. Lifestyle Apps: These apps, such as health and fitness, food and drink, and travel apps, are aimed at increasing and boosting the quality of life.
3. Social media applications: These applications let users interact with one another, post pictures and videos, and keep up with current events in real-time.

4. Productivity Apps: These apps, which include note-taking apps, email and messaging apps, calendar and scheduling apps, and others, help users manage their time and work more effectively.

5. Entertainment Apps: These apps, which include e-book readers, game apps, and music and video streaming apps, are made for leisure and entertainment.

6. Game Apps: These apps are devoted to giving customers enjoyable and captivating gameplay experiences across a variety of genres, including simulation, adventure, and puzzle games.

Numerous mobile apps are available on the App Store to meet your requirements and interests, whether you're trying to learn something new, keep in touch with friends and family, or are just looking to have fun.

iPhone users may search for and download apps to improve their experience via the App Store. There are tabs on the App Store UI for Today, Games, Apps, and Updates. The Today tab offers a daily curated list of new and featured apps, along with biographies of the developers. Categories such as Top Charts, Categories, and Explore are displayed in the Games and Apps tabs.

The Updates page, last but not least, shows any updates that are accessible for your installed programs.

To find apps in the App Store, use the search bar at the bottom of the screen. Additionally, you can narrow down your search results by choosing from groups like Games, Business, Education, or Entertainment. Your search results can also be sorted by relevance, rating, or release date. You can locate the ideal software that satisfies your particular needs by filtering and sorting the results.

The procedure for downloading and installing apps from the App Store is simple. To begin the download, just click the Get button next to the app's name. The software will automatically download if it is free. Using your Apple ID and password or another payment method, such as Apple Pay, you must confirm the purchase if the app is paid for. The app will start downloading instantly when you confirm your purchase. The downloaded software will show up on your home screen and be accessible.

In order to make sure that your apps function properly and effectively, managing app updates is important. To check for updates, go to the Updates tab on the App Store interface. If there are any updates available, an Update button will appear next to each app. Tap the Update icon to download and install the latest version of the app. As an alternative, you can activate all of your apps' automatic updates in the App Store's settings.

Apps can be downloaded and installed on iPhones through the App Store, a user-friendly platform that expands the capabilities of the smartphone. Users can quickly locate the software they require by utilizing the search and filter options, and by keeping their apps updated, they can make sure that their smartphone operates smoothly and efficiently.

SETTING UP AND ORGANIZING YOUR APPS FOR EASY ACCESS

Keeping Your Apps Organized in Folders

You can find the apps you need more quickly and simply if you keep your iPhone's app collection organized in folders. Here are some easy steps to assist you in organizing your apps:

1. Tap and hold an app until it begins to jitter in order to create a folder.
2. To add the app to another app you desire in the folder, drag it onto that app. Release your finger once the folder has been made.
3. Give your folder a name by tapping the title and then entering the desired name.

4. To add additional apps, tap and hold an app until it begins to jitter before dragging it into the folder.

5. After opening the folder, tap and hold an app until it jiggles to remove it. Drag the app out of the folder to move it to the home screen.

6. To move the folder, tap and hold it until it begins to jitter. Drag it to a different location, then let go of it.

Additionally, you may quickly categorize your apps by using a secret technique. This is how:

1. Press and hold an application button until it wiggles.

2. Tap the other apps you wish to add to the same folder without raising your finger.

3. Drag all of the chosen applications to the new location. Then let go of your finger.

4. The chosen apps will be instantly added to the folder that is formed. By tapping on the folder's title and then entering the desired name, you can give it a name.

On your iPhone, you can keep your apps organized and easy to find by following these few recommendations.

Tips for Arranging Your Apps to Make Them Easier to Find and Use

It can be simpler to find and utilize apps on your iPhone if they are organized. Here are some guidelines for organizing your apps:

1. Arrange your dock: Regardless of the screen you are viewing, the dock is the bottom row of icons that is always visible. An app can be arranged by dragging it to the dock after being pressed and held until it jiggles. Additionally, dragging an app out of the dock will uninstall it.

2. Include widgets: Widgets offer rapid access to specific app features or data without opening the app. Swipe right from the home screen to open the Today View, scroll down, then touch Edit to add widgets. The widgets can then be added, removed, or rearranged as you see fit.

3. Reset your Home Screen layout. This will put all of your apps in alphabetical order, but it will also reset any custom changes you have made to your Home Screen, such as app folders or custom icon layouts. To reset your Home Screen layout, follow these steps: Go to Settings > General > Transfer or Reset iPhone > Reset >

Reset Home Screen Layout. Tap Reset Home Screen to confirm.

4. Remove unnecessary apps: Press and hold an app until it jiggles, then hit the X icon in the top-left corner of the app icon to eliminate pointless apps. You can view a list of your installed apps and how much storage they are using by going to Settings > General > iPhone Storage. You can then delete any programs you no longer require.

5. Add a folder to the dock: To add a folder to the dock, hold down the button on the folder while dragging it to the dock. The apps can then be added to the folder to maintain organization.

6. Use the search bar to find apps: From the home screen's center, swipe down to see the search bar. The app you're looking for will then show up in the search results when you input its name.

7. Add new apps to the App Library: If you want to just download new apps for the App Library, go to Settings > Home Screen and select "App Library Only" under "New App Downloads." By doing this, all new apps will be sent to the App Library rather than being added to your home screen. From the final page of your home screen, swipe right to open the App Library.

You can simply organize your apps and clean up your home screen using these methods, which will make it simpler to find and utilize the apps you need.

Using the App Library

The iPhone has a function called the App Library that categorizes your apps for you automatically, making it simpler for you to find and use them. This is how to apply it:

- To access the App Library, swipe left from your home screen until you reach the last page.
- Your apps will be shown in the App Library under several headings, including Suggestions, Recently Added, Entertainment, Social, and more.
- You can either browse the categories to select a certain program or type its name into the search bar at the top of the screen.
- You can alter the location from which new apps are downloaded. Go to Settings > Home Screen > App Library Only to accomplish this. Instead of the home screen, the App Library will automatically add new apps.

Organizing Your Home Screen Pages

On an iPhone, you can access all of your features and apps from the home screen. The pages on your home screen can be organized as follows:

- The pages on your home screen can be accessed by swiping left or right to navigate between them. Swipe to the right until you see the last page dot to see all of your pages.
- To hide or erase a page, tap and hold any app on your home screen until the app icons start to jiggle. Touch the page dots at the bottom of the screen to see all of your pages. To find the page you wish to conceal or remove, swipe left or right from there. Choose to Remove Page or Hide Page by tapping and holding the page dot.
- Touch and hold any app on your home screen until the app icons begin to wiggle to reshuffle pages. After that, drag any page dot at the bottom of the screen by tapping and holding it.

Keep in mind that arranging your apps and home screen pages can help you discover what you're looking for faster and save you time.

This chapter discusses the importance of the iPhone's internet connection in today's digital world. It covers various features of the Safari web browser, including the Smart Search Bar, tab navigation, and Private Browsing. Additionally, the chapter provides information on how to customize Safari's start page, text size, and privacy settings, as well as how to delete browsing history and use iCloud to store and sync files across Apple devices. The following chapter will cover how to maximize productivity with the iPhone.

4

MAKING THE MOST OF YOUR TIME

If you own an iPhone, you are well aware of the benefits of using it to keep in touch with loved ones and to amuse yourself with a variety of games and apps. You might be surprised to learn that the iPhone is actually a potent productivity tool. You can do more in less time because of its cutting-edge features and functions, which also help you save time and work more effectively.

While many of us use our iPhones for entertainment and conversation, they can also be effective tools that enable us to accomplish more in less time. We'll look at a few strategies in this chapter for maximizing your iPhone's productivity.

USING SIRI AND VOICE COMMANDS TO SAVE TIME AND STREAMLINE YOUR DAILY ROUTINE

The virtual assistant Siri was developed by Apple Inc. for its iOS, iPadOS, watchOS, macOS, and tvOS operating systems. Since its initial release as an iPhone 4S feature in October 2011, it has gained popularity as a voice-activated command and dictation tool.

Siri is capable of carrying out a number of functions, including placing calls, sending texts, creating reminders, playing music, and even giving directions. To comprehend voice commands and take the right action in response, it uses natural language processing. You may operate your smart home appliances or place food orders from your favorite restaurant using Siri in conjunction with other iPhone apps.

If you want to install Siri on your iPhone, the process is straightforward. Do the following:

1. On your iPhone's home screen, tap "Settings."
2. Scroll down and select "Siri & Search."
3. To activate Siri using voice commands, turn "Listen for "Hey Siri" on.
4. To configure your speech recognition, follow the instructions.

5. Toggle "Press Side Button for Siri" if you want to use the side button on your iPhone to summon Siri.

6. If prompted, adhere to the on-screen directions to enable Siri suggestions while using an app, the lock screen, or both.

After you've finished, Siri is ready for use. You can activate it by either saying "Hey Siri" or then your demand while holding down the side button on your iPhone.

But bear in mind that for Siri to work properly, there must be an active internet connection. Therefore, when utilizing Siri, ensure your iPhone is plugged into a Wi-Fi or cellular network.

Siri is a flexible virtual assistant that responds to voice commands to assist you with a range of tasks. It's simple to set up, and once you have it, you can use Siri to simplify your life. So why not give it a shot and see how Siri can increase your efficiency and productivity?

Common Voice Commands to Use With Siri

With the help of your iPhone 14, Siri, a potent virtual assistant, can complete a variety of chores. Here are some instances of what Siri can do for you:

Waking Siri: To activate Siri on your iPhone, either say "Hey Siri" or hold down the side button. You can give

Siri instructions or pose a query after it has been engaged.

Calling Someone or Sending a Message: Siri can call someone or send a message on your behalf. Saying "Hey Siri, call John" or "Hey Siri, send Sarah a message saying "I'm running late" are a couple of examples.

Asking Questions: Siri can provide you with all kinds of information, from the most recent sports scores to the weather forecast. Such questions as "Hey Siri, what's the weather like today?" "Hey, Siri, who won the game last night?" are a couple of examples.

Searching your phone: Siri may be used to search your phone to find items such as certain emails or apps on your iPhone. As an illustration, you may ask Siri, "Hey Siri, find my photos from last weekend" or "Hey Siri, open the Facebook app."

Setting schedules: Siri can assist you in creating schedules and setting reminders. For instance, you may tell Siri to, "Hey Siri, schedule a meeting for tomorrow at 2 p.m." or "Hey Siri, remind me to call my doctor at 10 a.m. on Friday."

Getting Directions: Siri can provide you with instructions to your destination, whether you're driving or walking. You can ask Siri questions like, "Hey Siri, tell me how long it will take to get to the airport," or "Hey Siri, give me directions to the closest gas station."

Controlling Apple Music: Siri can control your Apple Music app, enabling you to play or pause music, create playlists, and do a lot more. For instance, you might tell Siri to play some Taylor Swift songs or to skip this.

With Siri, you can maximize the functionality of your iPhone 14. Siri can simplify and streamline your life, whether you're making a phone call, asking a question, or setting a reminder. Therefore, don't be afraid to give Siri a try and discover how it might assist you with your regular responsibilities.

HOW TO SET UP VOICE CONTROL

Siri vs. Voice Control

Siri and Voice Control are two voice-activated functions included with the iPhone. While Voice Control enables spoken commands to be used to operate your iPhone, Siri is a virtual assistant that communicates with your phone using natural language.

Despite the fact that both functionalities utilize voice recognition, their functions are different. While Voice Control is primarily made for users who might have physical restrictions or disabilities that make it challenging to engage with the touchscreen or other physical buttons on the device, Siri is designed to offer information, carry out tasks, and answer queries.

Through your iPhone's accessibility settings, you can easily set up voice control. Toggle the switch to the on position under Settings > Accessibility > Voice Control to enable Voice Control. Once activated, you can alter the commands that Voice Control understands and use them to operate your device without having to use your hands.

On your iPhone, for instance, you may use Voice Control to place calls, send messages, open apps, and change settings. Ask Siri to call a contact or send a message by saying "Hey Siri" to activate Siri. You can use voice commands such as "Open Messages" to open the Messages app, "Swipe down" to access your notifications, or "Go Home" to go back to your home screen.

In summary, Voice Control and Siri are both potent voice technology capabilities that can improve how effectively you use your iPhone 14. Voice Control is intended to help people with physical constraints with hands-free accessibility, whereas Siri is made for general use and everyday chores. You can get the most out of your iPhone and utilize it in ways you never imagined by learning to use both of its features.

You can write your own commands and alter the language of the Voice Control on your iPhone to fit your needs. With Voice Control, you may use voice commands instead of touch controls to complete a variety of tasks on your iPhone.

Create your own unique commands to personalize Voice Control. You can do any activity on your iPhone 14 with these custom commands, such as opening a certain app, taking a screenshot, or sending a message to someone. For instance, you might program a custom command to start your preferred music app whenever you say, "Play my music." The steps below can be used to configure custom commands:

1. Select Settings, followed by Accessibility.
2. Select Customize Commands after selecting Voice Control.
3. Press "+" to add a new command.
4. In the "Phrase" section, enter the phrase you want to use as a custom command.
5. In the "Action" area, choose the action you want Voice Control to carry out when you utter the order.

With Voice Control, you may also alter the language, which is another personalization choice. You can modify the language that Voice Control responds to if you speak a different language. To switch the language, do the following:

1. Select Settings, followed by Accessibility.
2. Tap Language, then Voice Control.
3. Select the language you want to use from the list of available options.

You can make your iPhone more useful and accessible by personalizing Voice Control. Voice Control can be customized to meet your own requirements and preferences using custom commands and language settings.

MANAGING YOUR CALENDAR FOR MAXIMUM PRODUCTIVITY

The iPhone 14's Calendar app makes it simple to manage your schedule and remember key dates. The flexibility to see your calendar in various ways according to your needs is one of this app's most helpful features.

Your events are displayed in chronological order in the List view, with the most recent event appearing at the top. Select the language you want to use from the list of available options.

The Daily View displays each of your daily events. This view is useful for taking a close look at your daily schedule and making sure you're on track.

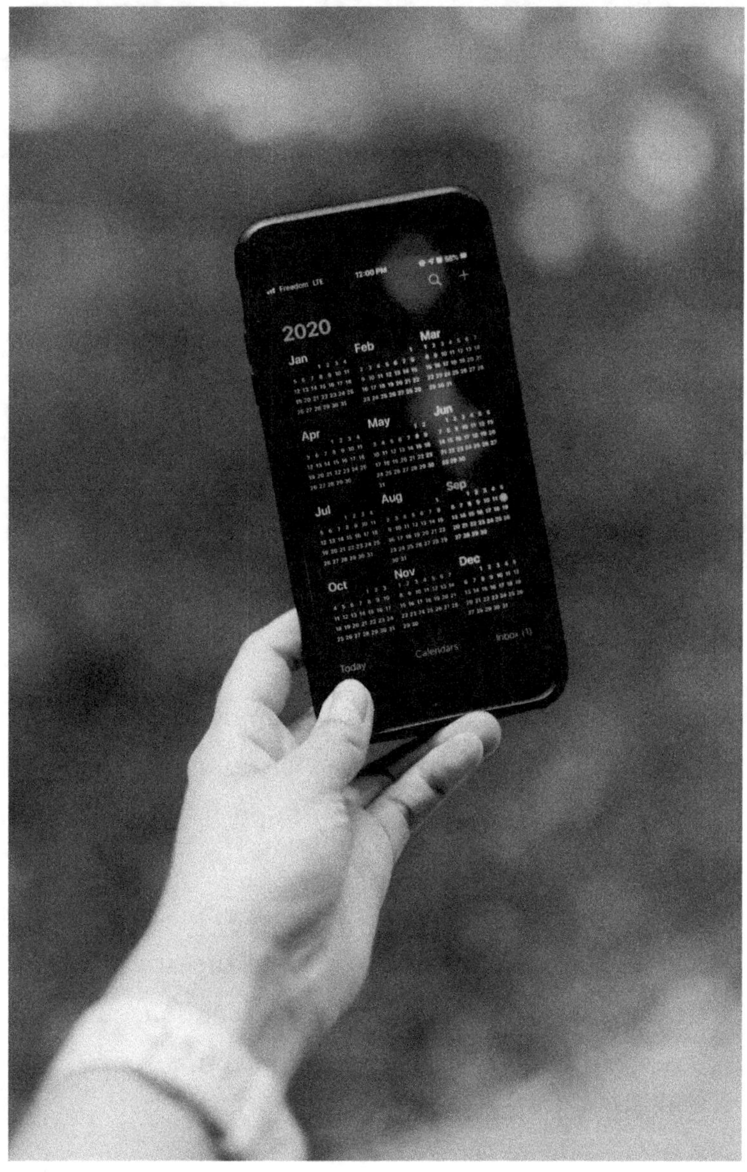

All of your upcoming events are shown in the Weekly view. This view is useful for getting a comprehensive picture of your schedule and locating any conflicts or openings.

Your complete month's schedule is displayed in the Monthly view. This view makes it easy to see all of your events at once and make future plans.

Your full year's worth of events is displayed in the Yearly view. Important dates like birthdays, holidays, and anniversaries can be seen with this view.

Simply open the Calendar app and tap on the relevant tab at the bottom of the screen to access these various calendar views. Additionally, you can swipe left or right to change views. You can effortlessly manage your time and stay on top of your schedule with your iPhone by changing your calendar layout.

Your iPhone's Calendar app has a number of functions that can help you effectively manage your calendar. The best features and usage tips for the app are listed below:

1. Tap the "+" symbol in the Calendar app and enter the event's specifics, such as the time, place, and date. Additionally, you can schedule repeating activities like weekly meetings or monthly appointments.

2. Tap on the event you wish to alter, then choose "Edit Event." Any necessary revisions can then be made and saved.

3. To remove an event, swipe left on it and select "Delete."

4. To find a particular event, utilize the Calendar app's search feature by tapping the magnifying glass icon at the top of the screen and inputting the necessary keywords.

5. Using notifications and reminders can help you avoid missing a crucial event. To establish an alert, tap on the event and select "Alerts." You have the choice of getting a notification before, during, or after the event.

6. When you add someone's birthday to your Contacts app, their birthday will automatically appear in your Calendar app. To make sure you don't forget to send a birthday greeting, you can also set a reminder.

7. You can create events with Siri without opening the Calendar app. Just activate Siri and say something like, "Create a meeting with John at 3 p.m. on Monday."

8. In the Calendar app, you can easily drag events to a different day or time period to organize them.

9. It's simple to share happenings with others. To invite people to the event, just tap on the event and choose "Invitees." Selecting "Add Person" and entering another person's email address allows you to share your calendar with them as well.

10. You can alter this in the options if you'd rather begin your week on a different day than Monday. Choose the preferred day by going to Settings > Calendar > Start Week On.

11. You can better manage your time by arranging events that take travel timing into account. Enter the event information and choose "Travel Time" to do this. The Calendar app will then alter the event start time in accordance with the travel time you enter.

Your iPhone's Calendar app offers a variety of options to help you properly manage your calendar. You can make sure you never miss a significant occasion and keep on top of your hectic calendar by utilizing these tools.

SIMPLIFYING LIFE WITH IPHONE SHORTCUTS

Users of the iPhone can create unique shortcuts for a variety of tasks with the Shortcuts app, a potent automation tool. The Shortcuts app allows users to automate a variety of actions and procedures on their iPhone, from sending a message to quickly activating an app or setting.

Users can adapt the pre-built shortcut templates in the Shortcuts app to their specific requirements. Using a straightforward drag-and-drop interface, users can also construct their own unique shortcuts, which makes the procedure simple to understand. Users can also send links to their shortcuts or publish them on the Shortcuts Gallery in order to share them with others.

Users of the iPhone can construct shortcuts that utilize information from other apps thanks to the Shortcuts app's integration with other iPhone applications. For instance, a user can design a shortcut that displays weather data on their iPhone's home screen after retrieving it from a weather app. Users may use the Shortcuts app to automate routine chores, saving them time and effort, and the options are essentially unlimited.

Below is a detailed description of each feature of the Shortcuts app.

Adding Shortcuts from the Gallery: You can add pre-made shortcuts to your iPhone using the built-in gallery that is included with the Shortcuts app. To add a shortcut from the gallery, open the Shortcuts app and choose "Gallery" from the bottom of the screen. Browse the many categories to find the shortcut you wish to add. By selecting "Add Shortcut," you can add a shortcut to your Library.

Making Your Own Custom Shortcuts: If there isn't a shortcut available that meets your needs, you can make your own. Activate the Shortcuts app, then select "Create Shortcut." Give your shortcut a name and a choice of icon. Tap "Add Action," choose an action from the list that appears, and add it to your shortcut. A series of tasks can be added that will be carried out when the shortcut is executed. When you're done adding activities, press "Done" to store your own shortcut.

Creating Automated Shortcuts: Automated shortcuts are shortcuts that are launched at predetermined times or locations in response to particular occurrences. To create an automatic shortcut, launch the Shortcuts app and choose "Automation" from the menu at the bottom of the window. Determine the trigger type you wish to employ, such as "Arrive" or "Leave," and then pick a location. Select the action you wish to take when the trigger is engaged by tapping "Next" after doing so. When finished, tap "Done" to save your automated shortcut after adding any further actions.

Running Shortcuts: To operate a shortcut, launch the Shortcuts app and press on the desired shortcut. As an alternative, you can add a shortcut to the Shortcuts widget or your home screen for quick access. The ellipsis (...) in the top-right corner of the shortcut must be tapped in order to choose "Add to Home Screen" or "Add to Widgets."

Adding a Widget for Shortcuts: A widget for Shortcuts is included in the software, and you may add it to your iPhone's home screen. Your most frequently used shortcuts are shown in the widget, making it simple to use them with a single press. On the home screen of your iPhone, swipe to the right to get the Today View, then scroll to the bottom of the page and press "Edit." Tap the "+" next to the Shortcuts widget to add it to your Today View.

Editing and Organizing Shortcuts: To modify a shortcut, open the Shortcuts app and tap on the shortcut you wish to change. In the shortcut's top-right corner, tap the ellipsis (...) and choose "Edit Shortcut." From here, you can modify the shortcut by adding, deleting, or rearrangement actions. By tapping "My Shortcuts" at the bottom of the screen, you can arrange your shortcuts by dragging and dropping them. By selecting "New Folder" and giving it a name, you may also create folders to organize similar shortcuts.

This chapter explains how to use Siri and voice commands to maximize productivity on your iPhone. It provides step-by-step instructions on how to activate Siri and examples of common voice commands, such as making calls and sending texts. The chapter also emphasizes the iPhone's potential as a productivity tool rather than just an entertainment and communication device. The next chapter will focus on the entertainment features of the iPhone.

Spreading the Word

"Knowledge is like money: To be of value it must circulate, and in circulating it can increase in quantity and, hopefully, in value."

— LOUIS L'AMOUR

How many times have you heard someone complain about how they don't understand their phone? How many stories have you heard about people running out of battery at the worst possible moment, or about the fear that their phone isn't private enough?

We live in a busy world, and technology moves fast… You're not the only one who hasn't been benefiting from the full potential of their iPhone.

My goal is to help as many people with their iPhones as I can… and as I'm sure you're aware by now, there are a lot of people out there looking for that information.

Luckily for you, you don't need to write a book to get it out there – that book already exists, and all I'm asking you to do is help me spread the word. Don't worry – it won't take more than a few minutes… and you don't even have to set foot outside your front door.

By leaving a review of this book on Amazon, you'll show other iPhone users where they can find all the information they need to get the most out of their devices.

Simply by letting new readers know how this book has helped you and what they'll find inside, you'll show them the value in discovering this information for themselves – and you'll let them know exactly where they can find it.

Thank you for your support. Now, let's get back to the task at hand!

Scan the QR code below to leave a review!

5

ENTERTAINMENT ON THE GO

This chapter highlights the entertainment features of the iPhone, including streaming movies and TV shows, listening to music, playing games, and taking pictures. The iPhone's high-quality display, audio capabilities, and computing power make it an excellent source of entertainment. The chapter provides tips on how to make the most of your iPhone for leisure and relaxation, making it the perfect device for unwinding after a long day or for entertainment on-the-go.

HOW TO USE THE CAMERA APP TO TAKE INCREDIBLE PICTURES AND VIDEOS

The Camera app on the iPhone is the ideal tool for taking pictures and films with the smartphone. Here are some guidelines for using the iPhone to take pictures and videos:

Opening the Camera app: Simply touch on the Camera icon on your home screen to launch the Camera app. As an alternative, you can use the camera immediately by swiping left on your lock screen.

Taking photos: When ready to take a picture, point your phone's camera at the object and tap the white circle button that appears on the screen. This will snap a picture.

Zooming in or out: Using the pinch gesture on the screen, you may zoom in or out on a subject. To zoom in or out, pinch in or out.

Camera orientation: The Camera app may be used in either portrait or landscape mode, depending on how you are holding your iPhone. Depending on how you're holding your device, the app's orientation will change automatically.

Flipping the camera: To switch between the front-facing and back-facing cameras, tap the camera symbol that looks like two arrows in a circle. This is located in the screen's Lower right corner.

Taking screenshots: When using the Camera app, Press the home/right side power button, and volume up button quickly.

Different camera settings: The Camera app has a number of settings that can be utilized for various kinds of pictures. Some of the most popular modes are listed below:

- Video: This mode allows for the recording of videos. Simply tap the red circle button on the screen once to begin and end the recording.
- Time-lapse: This option allows for the creation of time-lapse videos. By continually taking photos, the camera will later compile them into a video. To begin recording, just hit the red circle button after tapping the time-lapse mode symbol.
- Slo-mo: Videos shot in slow motion are captured using this technique. Tap the red circle button after choosing the slo-mo mode icon to start recording.
- Pano: Panoramic images can be taken using this mode. To capture the picture, simply tap the

pano mode icon and then adhere to the on-screen directions.

- Portrait: A blurred background is employed while capturing portrait shots in this mode. Simply tap the icon for portrait mode to take the picture.
- Cinematic: Videos with a film-like appearance are captured in this setting. To begin recording, hit the red circle button after tapping the icon for cinematic mode.
- Square: Square photographs are captured using this setting. To capture the picture, just tap the square mode icon.

To sum up, the iPhone's Camera app is a simple-to-use tool for taking excellent pictures and films. You should be able to use your iPhone to capture excellent pictures after following these instructions.

Tips for Customizing Your Camera Settings for Different Scenarios

Customizing your camera settings on your iPhone 14 might make all the difference in getting the ideal photo. You can create beautiful pictures and films in a variety of situations by giving priority to faster shooting, lens correction, scene identification, and seeing outside the frame.

Let's start by concentrating on quicker shooting. Modern technology in the iPhone 14 makes it possible for quicker autofocus, greater low-light performance, and enhanced image stabilization. To make the most of these features, we advise using Burst Mode to record quickly moving objects like children, pets, or athletes in motion. Tap the red circle button after choosing the slo-mo mode icon to start recording. To record some motion and sound before and after the shot, you can enable Live Photos.

The next step in attaining the best image quality is lens correction. The built-in lens correction feature in the iPhone automatically corrects chromatic aberration, distortion, and vignetting. To guarantee your photographs are sharp and clear, you may also select "Enable Lens Correction" from the Camera Settings menu. With this setting, any lens flaws will be immediately fixed, producing sharper images with improved color accuracy.

Another excellent tool that might improve your photography in various lighting situations is scene detection. The AI in the iPhone 14 can distinguish between various scenes and change the camera settings accordingly. For instance, the camera will automatically adjust the exposure and color temperature if you're taking a picture of a sunset in order to capture the vivid hues of the sky. Go to the Camera Settings menu and turn on "Scene Detection" to enable this feature.

You can peek outside the frame on your iPhone, which completely changes how you compose photos. You may modify your composition and catch more of the scene thanks to this function, which allows you to view what's happening outside the frame. Go to the Camera Settings menu and turn on "View Outside the Frame" to activate this option. Once activated, you can adjust your camera to get the ideal photo by seeing a faint outline of what's going on outside the frame.

If you enjoy taking pictures, you might want to experiment with different photographic techniques to give your iPhone pictures a more artistic feel. The camera app on the iPhone 14 has a number of built-in styles that can help you create various moods and effects in your photographs, like vivid color, high contrast, and black and white.

To access the photographic styles, open the Camera app and then tap on the three overlapping circles in the top-right corner. By doing so, the Camera Settings menu will appear, from which you can choose "Photographic Styles." There are various choices available here, including "Standard," "Vivid," "Rich Contrast," and "Warm." Each aesthetic is intended to bring out a particular quality in your images, including color saturation, contrast, or warmth.

If the pre-existing styles, however, fall short of your requirements, you can design your own unique style. Choose "Customize" from the Photographic Styles menu to accomplish this. The contrast, saturation, brightness, and warmth settings can be adjusted to get an appearance that suits your preferences.

Additionally, you have the option of sharing and saving your personal style. To achieve this, select the unique style you developed from the Photographic Styles menu. Select "Save Style" by tapping the three dots in the upper-right corner. Next, you can decide whether to share your style with other iPhone users or keep it private by giving it a name.

HDR mode: High Dynamic Range, or HDR, is a photography technique that enhances the information in both light and dark portions of a picture. Open the Camera app, hit the HDR button, and choose "Auto" to activate HDR mode. In this manner, the iPhone will decide when to apply HDR based on the lighting circumstances.

Portrait mode: This option is made to take beautiful portraits with a blurred background, giving your subject a polished and artistic appearance. Open the

Camera app, and then swipe to the left until the "Portrait" option appears. Before snapping the picture, make sure your subject is in the right posture and has enough light.

Adjusting the exposure: Occasionally, a picture could look excessively bright or too dark. When you tap the screen while snapping a picture, a yellow box will emerge, allowing you to change the exposure. To change the brightness, swipe up or down until you achieve the desired exposure.

Grid lines: You can use grid lines to align your images and make a composition that is more evenly balanced. Grid lines can be turned on by going to Settings > Camera and selecting "Grid."

Burst mode: Burst mode enables you to quickly take a number of pictures, making it helpful for catching action images or selecting the best picture from a selection. Holding down the shutter button while taking a picture will cause the iPhone 14 to take a number of pictures in burst mode.

Live photos: Live photos allow you to create a little video clip along with your photo, bringing memories to life. In the Camera app, press on the three overlapping circles to activate "Live" and enable live photos.

Camera timer: When taking selfies or group shots, the camera timer is helpful. Select the desired time by tapping the clock icon in the Camera app to start the timer.

Mirrored front camera: Select "Mirror Front Camera" under Settings > Camera to make the front-facing camera mirror your image.

Disabling camera noise: In some circumstances, camera noise can be distracting or obtrusive. Go to Settings > Sounds & Haptics and turn off "Lock Sound" and "Keyboard Clicks" to silence the camera.

Geo-tagging photos: Organizing and sharing your images can be made easier by geo-tagging them, which lets you add location data to each image. Go to Settings > Privacy > Location Services and turn on "Camera" to enable geo-tagging.

Resetting camera settings: To restore your camera's factory default settings, navigate to Settings > Camera > Reset and choose "Reset Camera Settings."

Your iPhone camera offers a variety of cutting-edge settings and functions that might enable you to capture some very remarkable images and videos. You can unleash your imagination and record memories that will last a lifetime by experimenting with these capabilities and changing settings to fit various scenarios.

Editing Photos

The Shots app on the iPhone has a number of options to assist you in enhancing and perfecting your shots. Let's look at some of the various editing programs that are out there and how you may utilize them to enhance your images.

Simply tap on the picture you wish to alter, then tap the alter button in the top-right corner to launch the Photo Editor. You can access a variety of different editing tools from there.

You may change the saturation, contrast, and vibrancy of your photos with color changes to make them appear more vibrant or muted. To make these adjustments, utilize the sliders or select one of the preset filters in the Photos app.

You can improve the overall brightness and clarity of your photos by using the brightness and sharpness settings. If you have a shot that is excessively dark or grainy, these techniques can be extremely helpful.

Your photographs' appearance can be drastically changed with the use of filters. The Photos app offers a variety of filters, including black and white, vintage, and others. By tapping on a filter, you may apply it. The filter's intensity can then be adjusted using the slider.

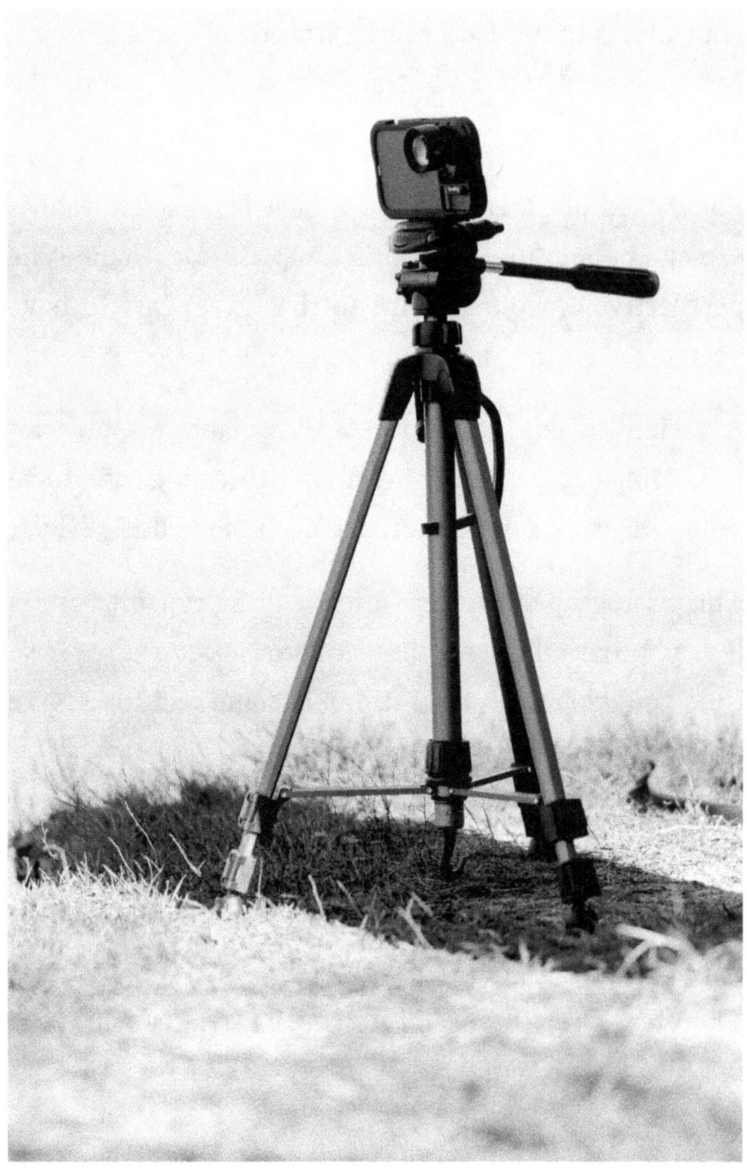

You can change the composition of your photographs by using tools for cropping and rotation. You can crop your photo to get rid of any extraneous parts, and you can use the rotate and straighten tools to change the angle.

For angled photography, the Adjust Perspective tool is extremely helpful. Using this tool, you can change the perspective of your picture so that it appears to have been taken from a different vantage point.

A variety of editing choices are available for portrait mode images, including the ability to change the focal point, the background blur, and even the lighting effect.

The photographs app also offers editing capabilities for live photographs, enabling you to select the precise time you wish to use the still image and add filters like loop, bounce, and long exposure.

You may enhance your photographs with a variety of strong editing tools included in the Photographs app. The Photos app includes the tools you need to change your photos' color, brightness, or composition. Therefore, use these editing tools to transform your photos into stunning works of art.

USING THE WALLET APP AND APPLE PAY FOR SECURE AND CONVENIENT PAYMENTS

Users can save and manage various kinds of digital passes, tickets, and payment methods using the pre-installed Wallet app on iPhones. By enabling users to save and retrieve their physical cards and tickets straight from their devices, the software eliminates the need to carry them around.

The Wallet app has storage space for many different passes, including boarding permits for flights, tickets to events, loyalty cards, and more. Passes can be manually entered into the Wallet app by the user or added by scanning a barcode or QR code.

The Wallet app can be used to store and manage credit and debit cards for Apple Pay, Apple's mobile payment system, in addition to passes. Using their iPhone, Apple Watch, or iPad, customers may use Apple Pay to make payments in-person, online, and within apps.

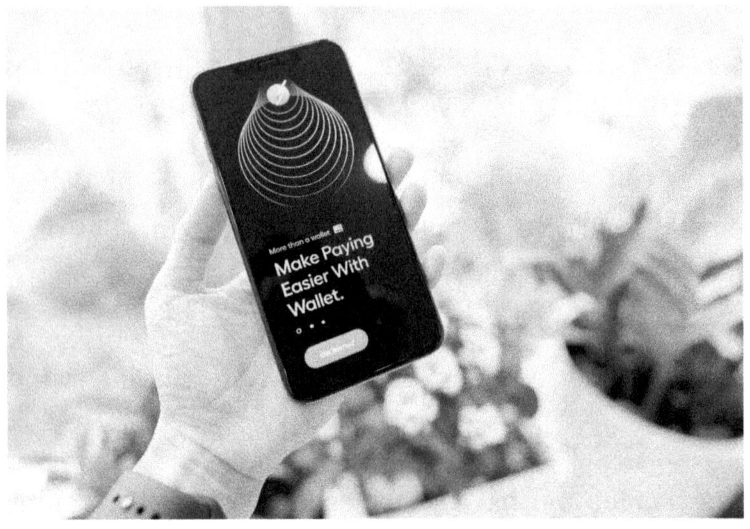

As well as having several helpful features, the Wallet app allows you to receive reminders for forthcoming events or flights and can display passes on the lock screen for quick access. Overall, the iPhone's Wallet app is a useful tool for centrally organizing all types of digital passes and payment methods.

A fantastic way to make secure payments and protect your financial information is by setting up Apple Pay on your iPhone. With Apple Pay, you may use your iPhone or Apple Watch to make purchases of goods and services. As it employs the security capabilities of your device to safeguard your information, it is a practical and secure method of payment.

You must first add your payment information in order to activate Apple Pay on your iPhone. You can do this by using the Wallet app, which is pre-installed on your iPhone. You can either add credit or debit cards that have already been saved in your iTunes account, or you can add cards from participating banks.

You can use Apple Pay to make purchases both online and at stores that allow contactless payments after adding your payment information. Simply place your iPhone close to the payment terminal to use Apple Pay in a store, then use Face ID or Touch ID to verify the transaction.

You can use the Wallet app to store and access various digital cards and passes, including your driver's license, boarding pass or ticket, health or auto insurance card, and digital key, in addition to making payments. This can be done by either choosing the "Add to Wallet" option within the app or by using your iPhone's camera to scan a physical card.

By double-clicking the side button on your iPhone or tapping the card within the app, you can quickly access your passes after adding them to the Wallet app. Holding your iPhone in close proximity to a suitable reader will also work to present your passes.

The Wallet app on your iPhone is a strong tool for managing your digital cards and processing safe payments. You can organize your life and keep crucial information close at hand by setting up Apple Pay and adding your passes to the app.

FINDING AND USING MEDIA APPS FOR MUSIC, MOVIES, AND TV SHOWS

Navigating the iTunes Store

Open the iTunes app and take the following actions to access the iTunes Store on your iPhone:

1. Finding music, movies, and TV shows: Tap on the corresponding tab at the bottom of the screen to find music, movies, or TV shows. To find specific things or to browse the featured items, use the search bar.

2. Purchasing and downloading materials

Follow these procedures to purchase and download content:

- Tap the thing you want to purchase.
- Tap the Get or Price button, and then authenticate your purchase using Touch ID, Face ID, or your Apple ID password.

- Immediately following the completion of your purchase, your item will begin downloading.

3. Using or giving an iTunes and App Store gift card:

Use these methods to redeem or mail an App Store & iTunes Gift Card:

- Choose the "More" tab at the bottom of the screen.
- Click "Redeem Gift Card or Code" and type in your gift card number or promotional code. To give a gift card by email instead, select "Send Gift Card by Email."

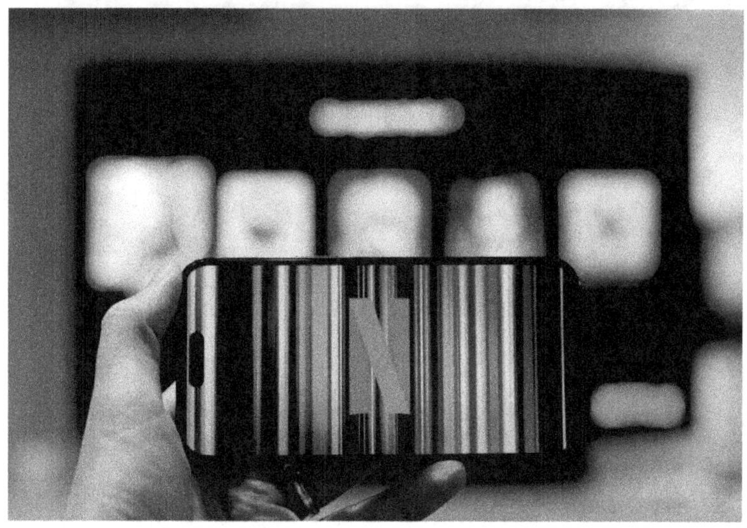

You can quickly navigate the iTunes Store on your iPhone 14 and take advantage of all the available content by following these instructions.

Using the Music App

You can utilize the built-in music app if you have an iPhone 14 with you. Here are some pointers for using the Music app and navigating its menus.

1. Different tabs: There are numerous tabs available in the Music app, including Top Picks, Recently Played, Made For You, Stations For You, Replay, and Listening Now. You can find your favorite music on these tabs, learn about new musicians and musical styles, and quickly access the tracks you've recently played.

2. Browsing: You can look through a variety of categories, including Genres, On the Air 24/7, City Charts, New Music, Videos, Featured Playlists, and New Music. You can find music quickly using this function, as well as find new songs and playlists.

3. Radio: The Radio option offers access to numerous live radio stations and stations that have been specially selected based on specific genres and artists. Additionally, you can design

your own station based on your preferred musicians or songs.

4. Library: All of the downloaded music, including Playlists, Artists, Albums, Songs, Videos, Genres, Compilations, and Composers, may be found on the Library tab. Additionally, this page has access to Recently Added and Downloaded Music.

5. Search: You may quickly find any song, artist, album, or playlist using the search feature. Browse the results after entering the search term.

6. Microphone: While using other apps, you can manage your music playback using the Mini Player feature. You may access this option by swiping up on the Now Playing screen.

7. Song Playing tips: Simply look through your music library or do a search to start playing a song. Once you've located the music, you can tap it to start it playing. You may download it for offline listening or include it in a playlist.

You can locate, stream, and download your preferred music on your iPhone 14 with the help of these tools. It's simple to listen to your favorite musicians and find new ones with the Music app.

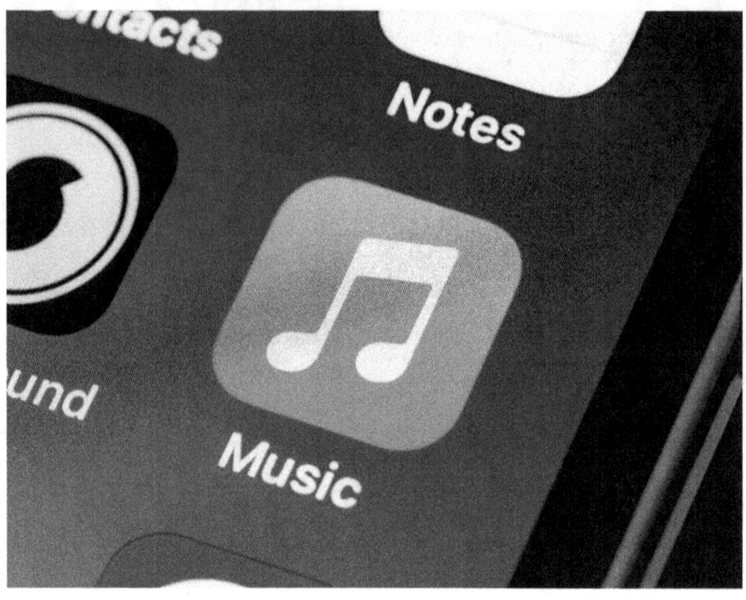

Apple Music, a music streaming service with a huge catalog of songs, playlists, and radio stations, is available to iPhone users. You can access only Apple Music material, make playlists, and listen to music offline. You must, however, keep in mind that Apple Music is a premium service, so you must sign up in order to use all of its features.

The Apple Music subscription process can be started by opening the Music app on your iPhone, tapping the "For You" button, and choosing "Try it Now" or "Get Started." New users of Apple Music receive a three-month free trial before being billed on a monthly basis. Through the App Store or iTunes, you may also become an Apple Music subscriber.

After signing up for Apple Music, you can begin browsing its enormous collection of songs, playlists, and radio stations. You can find new music by using the app's many tabs, which include Top Picks, Recently Played, Made For You, Stations For You, Replay, and Listening Now. By choosing the "Browse" option, you can also browse through various genres, featured playlists, and new releases.

On Apple Music's radio feature, you can make your own personalized radio stations based on your favorite musicians or songs or tune in to live radio stations. The "Library" option also gives you access to your personal music collection, which contains playlists, musicians, albums, and songs. You may look up certain songs, artists, or playlists using the "Search" tab, and the "Mini Player" function lets you manage your music playback as you explore other apps.

Using SharePlay to Stream Media and Play Games With Friends and Family Over FaceTime

The iPhone comes with a feature called SharePlay that enables FaceTime gaming and media streaming with friends and family. It is a fantastic way to stay in touch and exchange stories with loved ones who might not be nearby.

To use SharePlay, you must first be on a FaceTime chat with the person you wish to share with. Once on the call, tap the SharePlay icon at the bottom of the screen to launch SharePlay.

Simply start a group conversation with the people you wish to SharePlay with in order to use SharePlay in messages. Next, select what you wish to share by tapping the SharePlay symbol in the message thread.

During a FaceTime chat, you may also use SharePlay to share music with other people. When on a call, press the SharePlay icon, choose the Music app, and then select the song you want to share.

Watching videos together is also possible when using SharePlay during a FaceTime conversation. Tap the SharePlay icon, choose the TV app or another video app, and then pick the video you wish to watch in order to watch it together. The video will then begin playing for both you and the person you are sharing it with.

Screen-sharing is another great SharePlay function. FaceTime calls allow you to share your screen with others, making it simpler to collaborate on projects or instruct someone on how to use their device. By tapping the SharePlay icon, choosing the Screen option, and then deciding whether to share your complete screen or simply a certain app, you can share your screen with others.

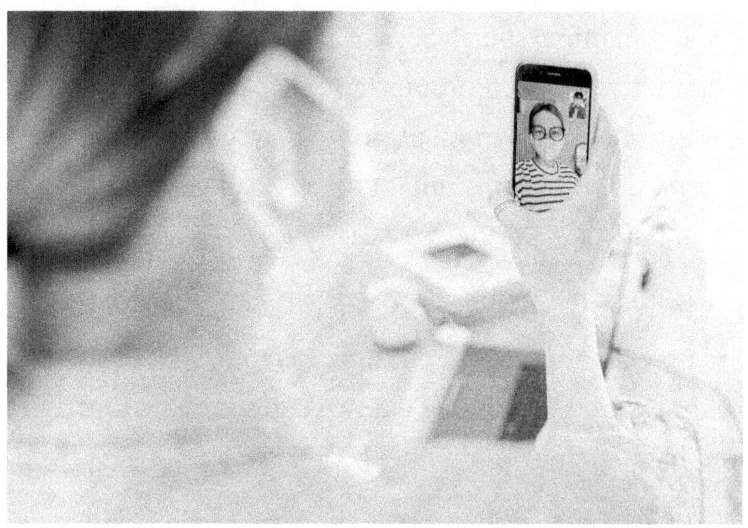

Additionally, when on a FaceTime call, you can use SharePlay to play games in Game Center with other people. Tap the SharePlay icon, choose Games from the menu, and then select the game you wish to play. You can begin playing with the person you are sharing the game with once the game has been chosen.

In summary, SharePlay is a fantastic tool for maintaining relationships with friends and family, whether you want to share material, work on projects together, or play games.

STAYING ENTERTAINED WITH GAMES AND OTHER APPS

Apple's gaming social network, Game Center, enables iPhone users to communicate with friends and other players. It gives you a place to play games, challenge others, collect achievements, and keep track of your progress.

Go to your device settings, tap on your Apple ID, then tap on Game Center to configure Game Center on your iPhone. You may enable Game Center, create a profile, and log in using your Apple ID here.

Select the "Create Profile" option and provide the required information, including your username, profile photo, and bio, to establish a Game Center profile. This will make it easier for you to locate and communicate with your platform buddies.

Adding friends to Game Center is easy. Launch the Game Center application, choose "Friends" from the tabs, and then hit the "+" button. By inputting their Game Center username or email address, you can add your friends here. In a similar manner, swipe left on a friend's name and select "Remove."

After adding friends, you can issue a game challenge to them. To challenge a buddy, just choose the game you wish to play, tap on that friend, and then hit "Challenge." Once your friend accepts the challenge, you can begin playing. Your friend will be notified of it.

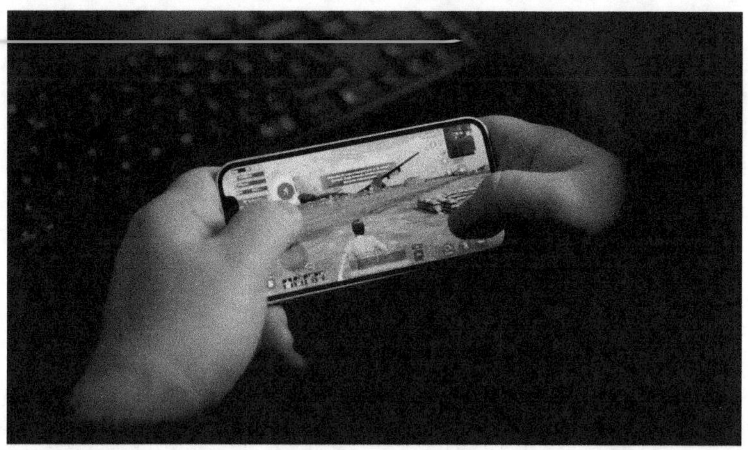

When playing games on your iPhone, Game Center is a terrific way to socialize with other players, challenge your friends, and have fun. It's no surprise that it's a well-liked social gaming platform with its user-friendly UI and fun features.

Looking for entertaining iPhone games to play? Games are simple to find and download from the App Store. How to begin is as follows:

1. Access the App Store: On your iPhone's home screen, tap the App Store icon.
2. Search for games: Use the search box at the bottom of the screen to look for games by name

or browse the various game categories that are offered. For popular and trending games, you may also look in the featured games section of the App Store.

3. Get information on games: To reach a game's page after finding one you want to play, tap on its emblem. You can read the game's description, view pictures and videos, and examine user reviews and ratings here. This might help you evaluate if a game is right for you before downloading it.

4. Download games: On the game's page, click the "Get" or "Download" option if you want to download the application. You must verify your purchase using your Apple ID and password, Face ID, or Touch ID if the game has a price. When the game is downloaded, your iPhone 14's home screen will display an icon for it.

Keep in mind that some games may demand an online connection or in-app purchases. Before downloading, make sure the game is something you'll love by carefully reading the description and user reviews. Enjoy exploring the plethora of games available on the App Store.

This chapter discusses how the iPhone can be used as an entertainment tool beyond its traditional business and communication functions. It covers various ways to utilize the iPhone's high-quality display, audio capabilities, and computing power, including streaming movies and TV shows, listening to music, taking photos, and playing games. The Camera app is also highlighted for capturing beautiful memories. The next chapter will focus on the health and fitness features of the iPhone.

6

FEATURES FOR TRACKING, MONITORING, AND IMPROVING YOUR HEALTH

Imagine carrying a device like the Star Trek Tricorder in your pocket that lets you keep tabs on your fitness and health. The Tricorder may still be a made-up device, but the iPhone is a close second. Your iPhone can help you stay on top of your physical and emotional health with its built-in health apps and functions. The different health-related functions and apps that the iPhone has to offer will be covered in this chapter, including how to measure your activity levels and even monitor your heart rate. By the end of this chapter, you will have the knowledge necessary to make the most of your iPhone as a useful tool for sustaining an active and healthy lifestyle.

THE IPHONE'S BUILT-IN HEALTH AND FITNESS FEATURES

The Health app on the iPhone is an effective tool for keeping track of your physical health and well-being. The Summary view, which gives you an overview of your health data, will be the first thing you see when you open the app. This includes any other data you have uploaded into the app, along with your daily step total, heart rate, and other vital indications.

There are various areas in the Summary view, including Activity, Mindfulness, and Sleep. Each part gives you a brief rundown of your health statistics and may be tailored to display the details that apply to you the most. To see more specific details about your health statistics, tap on any of these categories.

The Health app for the iPhone also has sections for sharing and browsing information in addition to the Summary section. Using the Sharing feature, you can divulge information about your health to other people or software programs.

This function is especially helpful for people who are keeping track of their health with the aid of a doctor or a personal trainer. These individuals can obtain individualized guidance and help by disclosing their health information.

On the other side, the Browse section enables you to go through several subcategories of health data. You can go through sections like "activity," "body measurements," and "vitals." You may use your iPhone to track a number of parameters within each category. Metrics like body weight, body fat percentage, and body mass index, for instance, are included in the category of body measures. You can measure these metrics to keep an eye on changes in your body composition and modify your food and exercise regimen as necessary.

Heart and hearing health categories can be found in the Browse area as well. You can track your exposure to loud noises and keep track of your hearing capacity over time by using the hearing category. Contrarily, the heart category contains measurements like blood pressure, electrocardiogram (ECG) data, and heart rate. You can monitor your cardiovascular health and spot any possible problems early on by keeping track of these parameters.

Let's take a deeper look at the various health categories the iPhone's Health app offers as we continue our exploration. Hearing, Heart, Body Measurements, Vitals, and Activity fall under these categories.

Let's start by thinking about the Hearing category. For people who are worried about hearing loss or who want to keep track of the impacts of exposure to high noise levels, this part is very beneficial. Users can measure the decibel level of their surroundings in this category and get alerts when the noise level is too high. Additionally, users can monitor their hearing health over time and track the volume of their headphones.

Moving on to the Heart category, this area of the app enables users to keep an eye on their heart rate, which is a crucial sign of general fitness and wellness. When a user's heart rate crosses a specified level, the app can notify them. The electrocardiogram (ECG) records, which can identify abnormal heart rhythms, can also be tracked by users.

Next, users can keep track of their physical characteristics, including weight, height, and body fat percentage, in the Body Measurements area. Additionally, users can keep tabs on how much water they drink each day and how well they sleep.

In the Vitals section of the app, users can monitor their blood pressure, blood glucose levels, and other important vitals. Those with chronic diseases like diabetes or high blood pressure will find this part very helpful.

Finally, the app's Activity area enables users to keep track of their daily physical activity, including the number of steps they take, how far they go, and the number of active calories they burn. Users can also create daily exercise objectives and monitor their success in meeting those goals.

SETTING UP AND USING THE HEALTH APP

Setting up your Health Profile

Open the Health app on your iPhone and select the "Browse" tab from the bottom to begin setting up your health profile. Then, press "Profile" and fill out the form with your details, including your name, birth date, sex, height, and weight.

Choose Your Favorite Categories to Track

By pressing the "Browse" option and navigating to the "Health Categories" section at the bottom, you can choose the categories you want to track. The categories you want to track can then be chosen from, such as "Heart," "Body Measurements," "Hearing," or "Vitals."

Adding Health Data

There are two ways to contribute health information to your Health app: manually entering the data or having your iPhone track it for you. You may connect your glucose meter to your iPhone to automatically track your blood sugar levels, for instance, or manually enter your blood pressure results.

Setting up a Medical ID

A Medical ID is an essential component of the Health app that enables you to enter critical medical data, including allergies, prescriptions, and emergency contacts. You may set up your Medical ID by tapping "Browse" and then "Medical ID." From there, fill out the necessary information and turn on the "Show When Locked" option so that first responders may readily access it even if your iPhone is locked.

Adding Third-Party Apps

The Health app also enables you to link up with a number of third-party applications that can assist you in tracking your exercise and dietary objectives. Go to "Browse" and choose "Apps" to look through the various alternatives before adding a third-party program. Tap "Get" to download and install the program once you've located it.

It's important to note that the Health app has extra functions when used with an Apple Watch, like the ability to track your daily activities and check your heart rate periodically. The Apple Watch may be used to keep track of your workouts and establish fitness objectives.

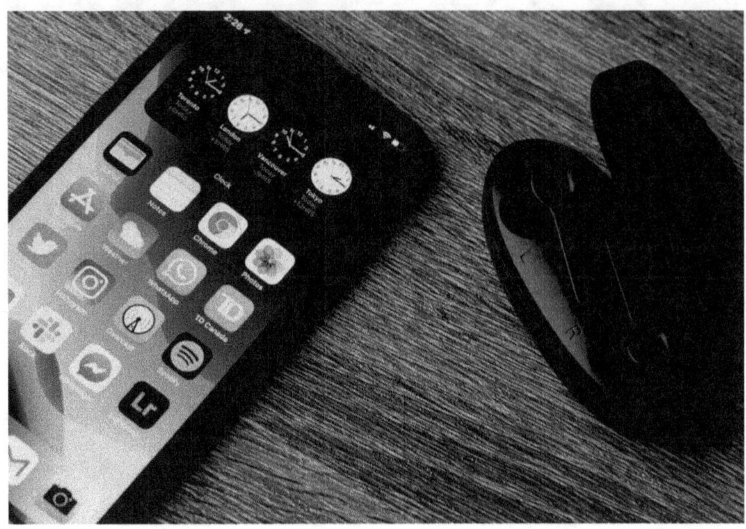

Regarding the next chapter, it's good to mention that the Health app stores sensitive health information, so it's important for users to take steps to protect their data. The chapter will likely cover features such as passcode and Face ID protection, as well as data encryption and control over which apps and devices have access to the Health app's data.

7

SECURING YOUR IPHONE AND PROTECTING YOUR PERSONAL DATA

This chapter emphasizes the significance of protecting your iPhone's data. To prevent unwanted access, it recommends establishing a secure passcode and using Face ID or Touch ID authentication. If your phone is lost or stolen, you can use Find My iPhone to locate it and remotely lock or wipe it.

To protect your personal information, use the built-in privacy controls, such as eliminating location monitoring and limiting ad tracking. It's also a good idea to check app access and back up your iPhone to iCloud or a computer on a regular basis. You can protect your iPhone and personal data by following these tips.

KEY SECURITY FEATURES ON THE IPHONE

Passcode Lock

One of the simplest yet most effective things you can do to safeguard the security of your iPhone is to set up a passcode lock. To open a phone with a password lock, the user must enter the passcode or utilize biometric authentication like Face ID or Touch ID. In the event that your iPhone is stolen or misplaced, this makes it harder for anyone to access your personal information.

The procedures below can be used to set up a passcode lock on your iPhone:

1. Open the "Settings" app on your iPhone.
2. Depending on the biometric authentication method you choose to use, scroll down and choose "Face ID & Passcode" or "Touch ID & Passcode."
3. If you have a passcode, enter it now.
4. If you haven't already, tap "Turn Passcode On" or "Change Passcode" to modify your current passcode.
5. You can either select a 6-digit or 4-digit passcode, or you can choose "Custom Numeric Code" to generate a passcode of any length.

6. If you have a Face ID-equipped iPhone, you may also choose to configure "Alternate Appearance" so that the device can detect your face even while you're sporting a mask or other facial covering.

7. You can add more fingerprints to an iPhone with Touch ID to increase detection and accuracy.

It's vital to keep in mind that you should choose a passcode that is easy for you to remember but difficult for others to figure out. Instead of utilizing straightforward codes like "1234" or "0000," pick one that is at least 6 digits long and contains a combination of numbers, letters, and special characters. Additionally, to guarantee ongoing security, update your passcode immediately if you ever have any reason to believe it has been stolen.

You can feel secure knowing that your iPhone and private information are better secured by setting up a passcode lock.

Touch ID

Use Touch ID to unlock your iPhone if it has a physical Home button and to verify your identity for other tasks. Using your iPhone is safer and easier with Touch ID because your fingerprint serves as your password.

To activate Touch ID on your iPhone, follow these steps:

1. Launch the iPhone's Settings app.
2. Tap "Touch ID & Passcode."
3. You must input your passcode if you have already set one up in order to proceed.
4. Click "Add a Fingerprint."
5. As instructed on the screen, press and lift your finger repeatedly from the Home button until your fingerprint is read.
6. You will be requested to set up Touch ID for use with Apple Pay, iTunes, the App Store, or both after your fingerprint has been properly captured.

Simply place your finger on the Home button to utilize Touch ID to unlock your iPhone or verify your identity. Make sure your Home button is dry and clean, and that you're using the right part of your finger if you're having difficulties utilizing Touch ID.

The iPhone 8 and prior generations are the only iPhones that support Touch ID because they have physical Home buttons. If you have an iPhone X or a later model, you need to use Face ID to unlock your device and confirm your identity. By following the directions in the Settings app's "Face ID & Passcode" section, you can configure Face ID.

You may increase the security of your iPhone and make it simpler to use by configuring Touch ID or Face ID on it. The elderly, who may have trouble memorizing long passwords or punching in passcodes, will find these capabilities to be of particular use.

Face ID

Face ID is one of the features that may be used to increase the security of your phone. This function uses facial recognition technology to authenticate purchases and unlock your phone. How to configure Face ID on your iPhone 14 is as follows:

1. Verify that the most recent iOS version is installed on your device.
2. Activate the Settings program on your iPhone 14.
3. "Face ID & Passcode" can be chosen from the list of options.
4. Tap "Set Up Face ID" and place your face in front of the front-facing camera by following the on-screen directions.
5. Turn your head in a circle to let the camera get multiple perspectives of your face.
6. After the scan is finished, select "Done."

7. At last, activate Face ID by clicking the toggle button next to "iPhone Unlock."

Remember that Face ID functions best when the phone is held at eye level and your face is clearly visible to the camera. This implies that you might have problems using Face ID to unlock your phone if you're donning sunglasses, a hat, or a face mask that covers a sizable area of your face. You can unlock your phone instead in these circumstances by using your passcode.

TIPS FOR SECURING AND PROTECTING YOUR IPHONE

Controlling What's Shown on the Lock Screen

A key aspect of safeguarding your personal information is having control over what displays on your iPhone's lock screen. Notifications, Siri suggestions, and other information can, by default, be seen on the lock screen and may possibly reveal private information. To reduce this danger, you can manage what is displayed on the lock screen.

Follow these instructions to change the settings for what appears on the lock screen:

1. Launch the iPhone's Settings app.
2. Click "Face ID & Passcode" or "Touch ID & Passcode," depending on how your device authenticates users.
3. When asked, enter your passcode.
4. Locate the "Allow Access When Locked" box by scrolling down.
5. To change what appears on the lock screen, a number of options can be switched on or off here. For instance, you can disable "Siri Suggestions," which displays app recommendations based on your usage patterns, and "Today View," which puts widgets on the lock screen.

You may avoid potentially sensitive information showing up on your iPhone's lock screen by changing these settings. If you frequently use your device in public or worry about illegal access to your personal data, this is very crucial.

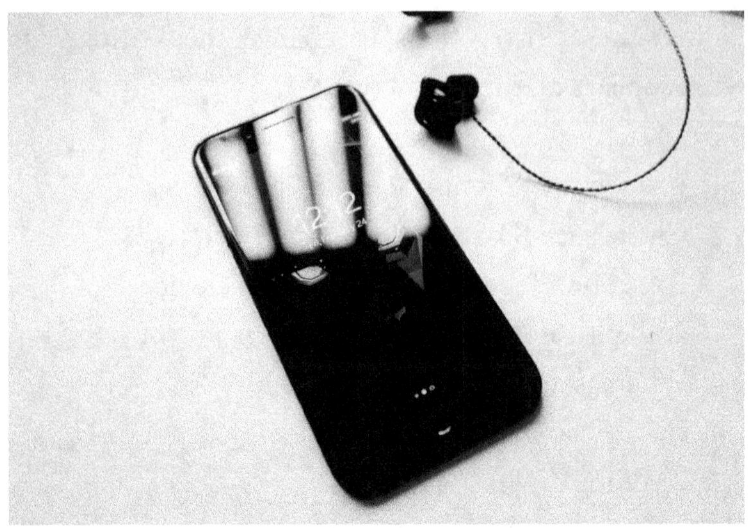

It's important to keep in mind, though, that while the device is locked, some functionalities might not be accessible. For instance, if you disable "Siri Suggestions" on the lock screen, Siri won't be able to open apps or carry out other actions without your iPhone being unlocked first.

Managing Privacy Settings

On the iPhone, controlling privacy settings is a crucial step in securing your personal information. Knowing and controlling what data is shared with third-party apps and services is essential, given the enormous quantity of personal information that may be saved on a smartphone.

Follow these procedures to manage privacy settings on your iPhone 14:

1. Launch the iPhone's Settings app.
2. Click "Privacy" to access the privacy options.
3. You can manage the privacy settings for a number of functions, including Location Services, Contacts, Photos, and more, in this section.
4. You can also toggle the access of apps to particular features on or off and check which apps have asked for access to them.
5. You can disable location access for an app, for instance, if you're worried about it tracking your location.

Regularly checking your privacy settings is crucial since certain apps may eventually ask for access to additional features or services. Additionally, you should be aware of any new privacy options that may be included in future iOS versions.

You may change your privacy settings to make sure that only trustworthy apps and services have access to your personal information. This is crucial if you are worried about privacy issues like identity theft or data breaches.

Managing Location Services Settings

An essential part of protecting your personal information on your iPhone is controlling the location services settings. On your iPhone, a lot of applications and services might request access to your location data by default, but you can choose which applications have access to this data.

Go to Settings > Privacy > Location Services on your iPhone to control location service settings. You can manage the apps' access from this page by viewing which ones have asked for access to your location data. Either fully disable location services or restrict access for each individual app.

To get accurate local forecasts, for instance, you might want to give your weather app access to your location data, but you might not want your social media applications to have this same access. You may have more control over how your location data is used and safeguard your privacy by modifying these settings.

It's also important to keep in mind that some applications may ask to access your location information even when you aren't using them. By changing each app's "Allow Location Access" setting, you can manage this. You have the option to either grant access whenever you are using the app or whenever you are not.

In general, controlling location services settings on your iPhone 14 can help safeguard your private information. You can make use of location-based services while simultaneously protecting your information by controlling which apps have access to your location data.

Limiting Ad Tracking

On the iPhone, limiting ad tracking is a crucial step towards protecting your privacy. By limiting ad tracking, you prevent apps from utilizing your data to deliver personalized ads, enhancing the privacy and security of your browsing. Go to your iPhone's settings, pick "Privacy," then press "Advertising" to enable this function. Then select "Limit Ad Tracking" from the menu.

It's important to keep in mind, though, that restricting ad tracking can occasionally hinder the functionality of some apps that depend on targeted ads to deliver a better user experience. If you restrict ad tracking, you might see more generic advertising and some apps might stop working properly. However, minimizing ad tracking is an essential measure for safeguarding your security and privacy.

In order to limit ad monitoring, you can also reset your Advertising Identifier. Advertisers use this particular identification to monitor your activities on many websites and apps. Resetting it allows you to start over and limits the data that is gathered about your browsing habits.

Check Passwords:

To keep your iPhone secure, you must use strong passwords. Go to Settings > Passwords to check the security of your passwords. You may see a list of all the passwords you've stored on your device here. Your iPhone will alert you if any of the passwords are insecure or duplicated so that you may take the appropriate precautions.

Find Your iPhone

If your iPhone is lost or stolen, the Find My iPhone feature might help you find it. Navigate to Settings > iCloud > Find My to turn this option on. Here, you may activate Find My iPhone, which enables you to view the location of your device on a map, remotely lock it, and, if necessary, erase its data.

Mail Privacy

You can also enable Mail Privacy to prevent tracking or monitoring of the content of your emails. Go to

Settings > Mail > Privacy Protection to turn on this function. You can activate the setting that masks your IP address from senders and blocks tracking pixels here.

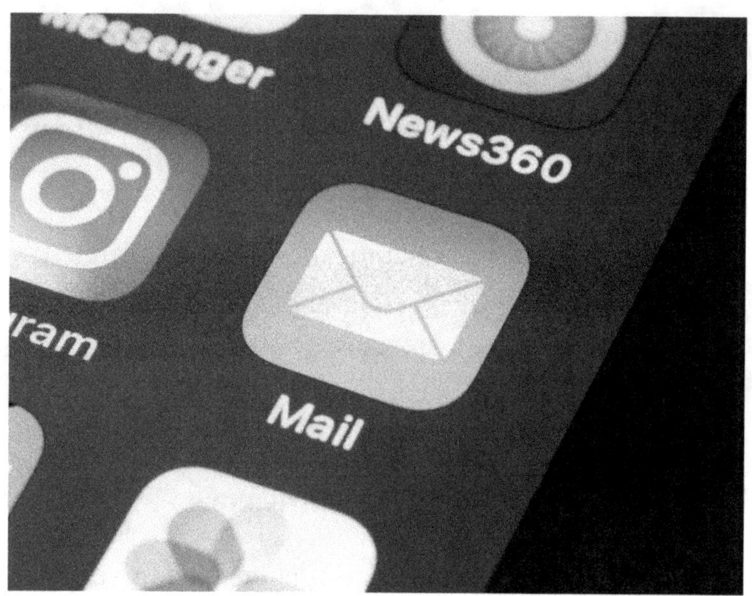

App Privacy Report

Navigate to Settings > Privacy > App Privacy Report to see which apps and how much of your device's data they are accessing. This feature gives you a thorough report on how each app has been utilizing the data on your smartphone and lets you modify the privacy settings for specific apps.

Securing Your Apple ID

Two-factor authentication

To protect your personal information, including your contacts, images, and payment information, you must secure your Apple ID. One of the best ways to safeguard your Apple ID is to enable two-factor authentication. This feature increases security and makes it more difficult for hackers to access your account.

To enable two-factor authentication for your Apple ID, open Settings and click your name at the top of the page. After that, select "Password & Security" and then "Turn on Two-Factor Authentication." Click "Continue" on the following screen to complete the configuration. Then adhere to the on-screen instructions.

When two-factor authentication is enabled, a verification code will be sent to a trusted device or phone number each time you sign into your Apple ID on a new device or browser. It is considerably more difficult for someone to access your account without your consent because this code is necessary in addition to your password.

Maintaining a strong and original password for your Apple ID is also crucial. Use a mix of upper- and lower-case characters, digits, and symbols, and avoid using the same password across numerous accounts. To create and store secure passwords, you can also utilize the built-in password manager on iOS.

This chapter emphasizes the importance of securing an iPhone and safeguarding personal data. Tips include creating a secure passcode, activating Face ID or Touch ID, and using Find My iPhone. Other privacy measures, such as disabling location monitoring, limiting ad tracking, and enabling two-factor authentication for Apple ID, are also discussed. Backing up data regularly is recommended. Chapter 8, which we will discuss next, provides insights into optimizing battery life.

8

STAYING POWERED UP

This chapter discusses the importance of maintaining your iPhone's battery and provides tips on how to keep it healthy throughout the day. It compares taking care of your phone's battery to maintaining your own energy levels and offers advice on changing behaviors and modifying settings to improve battery life. The chapter aims to help users avoid the stress of a dead battery during important activities.

HOW TO CHECK YOUR BATTERY USAGE

We want to make sure that our phone's battery can last as long as possible as we become more and more dependent on our iPhones for daily duties. Thankfully, the iPhone has a feature built into it that can help us maximize battery life. We'll show you how to access your iPhone's battery health recommendations in this section.

First, open your iPhone's Settings app and touch Battery. You can choose Battery Health from this menu. You should also activate Find My iPhone in order to remotely locate, lock, and wipe your smartphone in the event that it is lost or stolen.

If your battery health is nonetheless good, read down to the Battery Health section for advice on how to lengthen the life of your battery. The recommendations can involve turning on Low Power Mode, tweaking your settings, or figuring out which apps use too much power.

If you discover that your iPhone's battery life is not lasting as long as it once did, we strongly advise checking your battery health tips on a frequent basis. You can maximize the battery life of your phone and make sure it lasts as long as possible by paying attention to the instructions supplied by your iPhone.

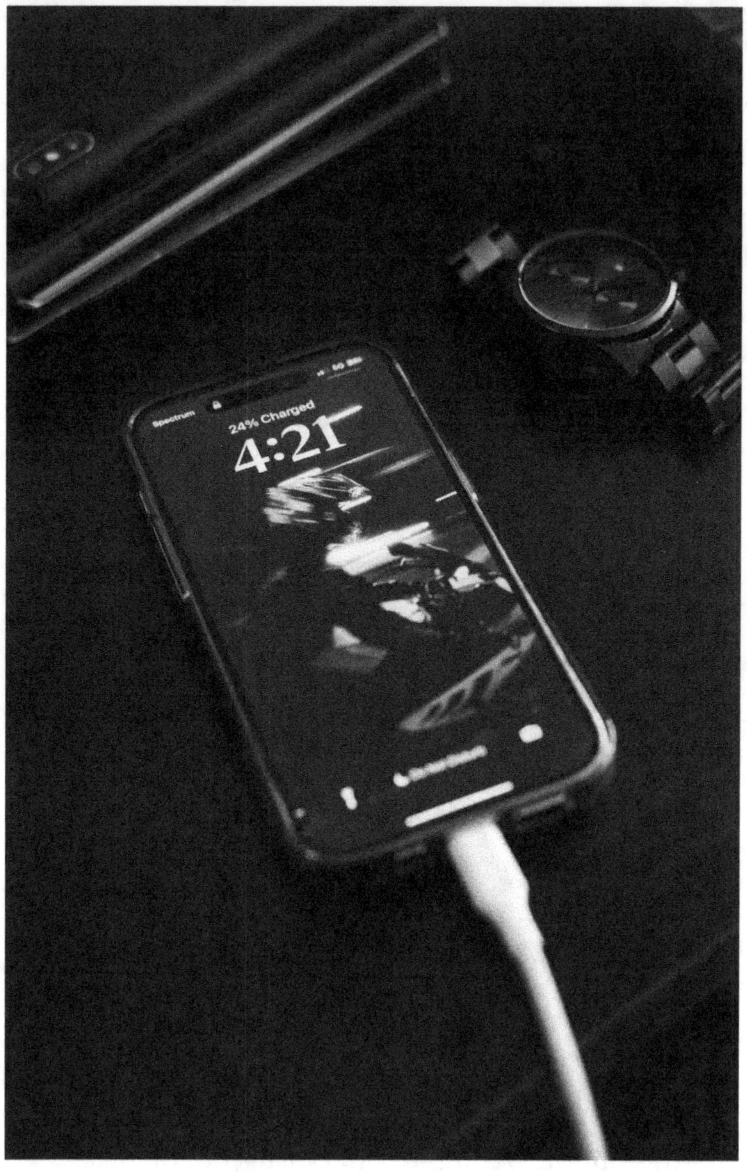

Your iPhone's battery settings can give you useful information on the condition and functionality of your device's battery. Let's walk through each battery-related function on the iPhone:

1. 1. Maximum Capacity of the Battery: This function lets you know how much power your iPhone's battery can hold when it is completely charged. Your iPhone's maximum storage capacity could get smaller as it ages. You might think about changing the battery if it falls below 80%.
2. Peak Performance Capability messages: This function lets you know how well your iPhone's battery is performing. You could come across a variety of messages, such as:

- Performance is normal: According to this notification, your iPhone is operating at peak efficiency.
- Performance management applied: According to this notice, your iPhone's performance has been slowed down in order to prevent unforeseen shutdowns. If you'd like your iPhone to operate more quickly, you can disable this option, but if the battery runs out of juice, your phone might shut down without warning.
- Battery health is unknown: This notification informs you that your iPhone is unable to

assess the battery's condition. You might need to get in touch with Apple Support to get more help.

- Performance management disabled: According to this notice, the performance management tool has been turned off.

- Battery health has substantially declined, and your iPhone's battery may need to be replaced, according to this warning.

- Important Battery Message: This message gives crucial details regarding the battery in your iPhone, such as when it needs maintenance or replacement.

You can take steps to extend the battery life and performance of your iPhone by keeping an eye on these Battery settings.

TIPS AND TRICKS FOR CONSERVING BATTERY LIFE AND MAXIMIZING PERFORMANCE

It can be difficult to keep your iPhone's battery charged all day. You may want to give a few methods a try in order to lengthen the life of your battery. Here are some suggestions to aid you:

1. Dim the screen: Lowering your screen's brightness can help you save battery life. By selecting Settings > Display & Brightness and sliding the slider to the left, you can change the brightness.

2. Use auto-brightness: You can also configure your iPhone to automatically adjust the brightness based on the available light. Turn on Auto-Brightness by going to Settings > Accessibility > Display & Text Size.

3. Turn off "Raise to wake": When you pick up or tap your iPhone, this feature activates the screen. Although useful, it can potentially drain your battery. You can disable the Raise to Wake feature by navigating to Settings > Display & Brightness.

4. Keep your apps updated: App updates frequently feature bug fixes and performance enhancements that can make your apps work more smoothly and save battery life.

5. Remove widgets: Although widgets might be useful, their frequent self-refreshing drains battery life. If you have widgets that are unnecessary, you might want to remove them.

6. Try restarting: Restarting your iPhone might occasionally help with battery drain concerns. Press and hold the Side button along with any

volume button once the power off slider appears. After shutting down your iPhone with the slider, press and hold the Side button once more until the Apple logo appears.

7. Turn off background app refresh: When you aren't using an app, it can continue to update its content in the background. It can be helpful, but it also uses up your battery. By navigating to Settings > General > Background App Refresh and flipping the switch, you can disable it.

8. Adjust location services for various apps: A number of apps use location services, which might decrease battery life. You may change the settings for each app individually by going to Settings > Privacy > Location Services.

9. Turn off "push notifications": One of the major causes of your iPhone's battery life being drained is push notifications. These notifications use a lot of battery and keep the screen active. Push notifications might reduce battery life, so turn them off. Navigate to Settings > Notifications and disable push notifications for any apps you don't want to get notifications from. The battery life can be considerably extended by doing this.

10. Set the auto-lock option to 30 seconds: Auto-lock is an additional feature that can prolong the life of your battery. Your iPhone's screen will automatically switch off after a predetermined amount of inactivity if you configure it to lock after a shorter amount of time. Your battery will last longer if you set the auto-lock time to 30 seconds. The auto-lock time can be changed to 30 seconds by going to Settings > Display & Brightness > Auto-Lock.

11. Avoid poor reception areas: Staying away from bad reception areas can also extend the life of your battery. When there is poor reception, your phone must use more power to search for a signal, which shortens the battery life. To help increase the battery life of your iPhone, make an effort to remain in signal-rich locations.

12. To turn off app specific alerts, follow these steps: Open your device's settings. Tap on "Notifications." Under "App notifications," find the app you want to turn off notifications for. Tap on the app name. Toggle off the "Allow notifications" switch.

You can make sure that your iPhone's battery lasts all day by using these suggestions to help it last longer.

UNDERSTANDING AND USING LOW POWER MODE

If you notice that the battery in your iPhone 14 is getting low, turning on Low Power Mode can help it last longer.

Certain iPhone capabilities will be temporarily disabled or altered to save battery life when Low Power Mode is activated. Automatic downloads, background program updates, and email fetching are a few of these features. As a result, updates and loading times for apps may take longer, but your device's battery life will be improved.

You can take the following actions to enable Low Power Mode:

1. Open your iPhone's settings.
2. Click Battery.
3. Switch to the Low Power Mode.

Activating Low Power Mode

When Low Power Mode is engaged, the battery icon in the top-right corner of your screen will turn yellow. Using Siri Shortcuts, you can also choose when Low Power Mode activates and deactivates. By employing the following steps while building a Shortcut, you can achieve this:

1. Open the Shortcuts app on your iPhone.
2. Tap the "+" icon to start a new Shortcut.
3. After choosing Add Action, search for "Low Power Mode."
4. Select "Set Low Power Mode."
5. Set the conditions under which Low Power Mode should activate and deactivate, such as when your battery reaches a specific point.

Remember that when Low Power Mode is on, some features will be changed or disabled, which could impact how well some apps run. But turning on Low Power Mode can be a useful technique to save power if you need to increase the battery life of your iPhone.

This chapter discusses how to keep your iPhone's battery healthy and maximize its performance. It goes over how to monitor battery usage, make use of built-in capabilities, and increase battery life. The following chapter will concentrate on specific features that help simplify the iPhone experience.

9

SIMPLIFYING YOUR IPHONE EXPERIENCE

This chapter strives to make the iPhone experience easier and more accessible for older people and their caregivers. The iPhone is a flexible device that fulfills the majority of users' demands, and this chapter looks at ways to make it more user-friendly for seniors, such as raising font size, using voice control, and enabling accessibility features.

The chapter uses real-world examples to show how to use the device's functions and offers tips on how to customize the iPhone for elders. Readers will have a better understanding of how to improve seniors' access to the iPhone and ensure they get the most out of their smartphone at the end of this chapter.

MAKING THINGS EASIER TO READ

The iPhone is a powerful device that can adapt to the needs of its users, and this includes making it easier to read. Whether you're an elderly senior or someone who just wants to maximize ease of use, there are a number of key features on the iPhone that can help you achieve this. We'll examine some of these features in more detail and discuss how to enable them in this section.

Magnifier

One of the most useful features for seniors is the Magnifier, which allows you to use your iPhone as a magnifying glass for physical written content. To activate the Magnifier, simply go to Settings, then Accessibility, and then Magnifier. Turn on the Magnifier feature, and you'll be able to zoom in on anything you want to read by triple-clicking the Home button.

Zoom

Another useful feature is Zoom, which allows you to magnify specific parts of the iPhone screen. To enable Zoom, go to Settings, then Accessibility, and then Zoom. Toggle on the Zoom feature, and you'll be able to zoom in and out of your iPhone screen by double-tapping with three fingers.

Display and Text Size

If you want to increase the font size of your iPhone, Display, and Text Size is the feature you need. Drag the slider to the right to enlarge the font size by selecting Settings, Display, and Text Size. This will enlarge and improve the readability of the text on your iPhone.

Speak Selection

Finally, there's Speak Selection, which reads out text or other screen content to you. Go to Settings, then Accessibility, and then Speech to use this feature. Turn on Speak Selection and you'll be able to highlight text and then tap the Speak button to hear it read aloud.

SIMPLIFYING TEXT MESSAGING

Text messaging is an essential feature on the iPhone, but it can be challenging for some users, especially seniors, to use comfortably. Fortunately, Apple has built several accessibility features into the iPhone's messaging app to make it easier to use. In this section, we will discuss three key accessibility features for simplifying text messaging on the iPhone.

Smart Typing

Smart Typing is an accessibility feature that helps users who have trouble seeing or reading small text. When enabled, this feature zooms in on the typing area to make it easier to read. To enable Smart Typing on your iPhone, go to Settings > General > Accessibility > settings-zoom, then toggle smart typing.

Predictive Text

Predictive Text is another useful accessibility feature for simplifying text messaging on the iPhone. When enabled, it suggests complete words and phrases based on the context of the message, which can help users complete messages faster. To enable Predictive Text on your iPhone, go to Settings > General > Keyboard, then toggle on Predictive.

Auto-Correction

Auto-correction is an accessibility feature that helps users quickly correct typos in their messages. When enabled, it automatically corrects common spelling mistakes and typos. To enable Auto-correction on your iPhone, go to Settings > General > Keyboard, then toggle on Auto-correction.

CUSTOMIZING HOW YOU INTERACT WITH YOUR IPHONE

As we mentioned in Chapter 4, Voice Control is a helpful feature that allows users to interact with their iPhone using only their voice. However, there are other special features that provide other helpful ways of using and interacting with the iPhone. In this chapter, we'll expand on the following iPhone accessibility features related to voice and sound:

VoiceOver: VoiceOver is a powerful feature that provides helpful hints and verbalizes on-screen content, making it easier for users with visual impairments to interact with their iPhone. To enable VoiceOver, go to Settings > Accessibility > VoiceOver and toggle the switch on.

Siri Voice Dial: Siri Voice Dial is a hands-free feature that lets you make calls verbally, making it easier for users with mobility or dexterity issues to place phone calls. To enable Siri Voice Dial, go to Settings > Siri & Search and toggle the switch on for "Press Side Button for Siri."

Audio descriptions: Audio descriptions provide spoken narration of what's happening in videos and movies, making it easier for visually impaired users to follow along. To enable audio descriptions, go to Settings > Accessibility > Audio Descriptions and toggle the switch on.

Assistive Touch: Assistive Touch is a powerful feature that makes it easier for users who have difficulty touching the screen to interact with their iPhone. With Assistive Touch enabled, users can perform gestures such as pinch, multi-finger swipe, and 3D Touch with a single tap. To enable Assistive Touch, go to Settings > Accessibility > Touch and toggle the switch on for "AssistiveTouch."

By utilizing these iPhone features, users can customize their experience and interact with their iPhone in ways that work best for them.

EMERGENCY FEATURES

The chapter provides information about various iPhone accessibility features that benefit users with messaging, voice and sound, and emergency situations. Both an explanation of the features and instructions on how to activate them are provided. The chapter also reminds readers about the Voice Control feature and the "Find My" feature. The next chapter will focus on troubleshooting common problems that users may encounter with their iPhones.

Emergencies can occur anywhere, at any moment, and without prior notice. Fortunately, iPhones offer a variety of accessibility features that can help you quickly and easily call for help, share your location, and get in touch with emergency contacts. In this article, we'll explore some of the most important iPhone emergency features, including emergency SOS, sharing locations, adding emergency contacts, and using lockdown mode.

Emergency SOS: Getting Help Quickly and Easily

Emergency SOS is an iPhone feature that helps you quickly call for help when you're in an emergency situation. Once enabled, you can press the side button five times in rapid succession to activate emergency SOS. This will instantly dial the emergency services number in your area and notify your emergency contacts that you require assistance.

To enable Emergency SOS on your iPhone, go to Settings > Emergency SOS and turn on the "Call with Side Button" and "Auto Call" features. In the same menu, you can also add emergency contacts.

Sharing Location

Sharing your location with others is another useful emergency function on the iPhone. This can be useful if you're lost, injured, or need help finding your way. You can also use this feature in conjunction with the "Find My" app (referenced in Chapter 3) to locate your iPhone if it's lost or stolen.

On an iPhone, select Share My Location under Settings > Privacy & Security > Location Services. The next step is for you to decide which contacts and for how long you wish to disclose your whereabouts.

Adding Emergency Contacts

You can add emergency contacts to your iPhone in addition to emergency SOS. These contacts will be notified if you activate Emergency SOS or if you add them to your Medical ID (referenced in Chapter 4). This can be especially useful if you have a medical condition or allergy that emergency responders need to know about.

To add emergency contacts to your iPhone, go to Health > Medical ID > Edit > Emergency Contacts. You can then add as many emergency contacts as you'd like and choose their relationship with you.

Lockdown Mode: Securing Your iPhone in an Emergency

Finally, Lockdown Mode is a new iPhone feature that was introduced in iOS 14.5. It's designed to help you quickly and easily secure your iPhone in an emergency situation, such as a protest, natural disaster, or other dangerous situation. When activated, Lockdown Mode disables Face ID and Touch ID and requires a passcode to unlock your iPhone.

To activate Lockdown Mode on your iPhone, go to settings-privacy & security lockdown mode.

This chapter explored emergency features available on iPhones, including Emergency SOS, Sharing Location, Adding Emergency Contacts, and Lockdown Mode. These features can help users quickly and easily call for help, share their location, and get in touch with emergency contacts in emergency situations. The next chapter will focus on troubleshooting common problems that iPhone users may encounter.

10

TROUBLESHOOTING COMMON PROBLEMS

This chapter discusses common problems that can occur with iPhones, such as freezing, overheating, Bluetooth, and connectivity issues, and provides step-by-step guidelines on how to troubleshoot and fix them. Although iPhones are generally reliable, they can still experience software bugs, hardware problems, and battery issues. By following the advice in this chapter, users can quickly and easily solve these problems and continue using their iPhones without interruption.

HINTS AND TECHNIQUES FOR RESOLVING TYPICAL IPHONE PROBLEMS

Users of iPhones may have difficulties and challenges when utilizing their devices, as with other technologies. Here are some of the most typical iPhone problems and solutions:

1. Black/White Screen of Death: occurs when your iPhone becomes unresponsive and only shows a black or white screen. If the problem persists, try forcing a reset of your device by simultaneously pressing and holding the power and home buttons for 10 seconds or until the Apple logo appears.

2. Overheating: Turn off your iPhone for a bit to let it cool down if it feels warm to the touch or if an overheating warning message appears. Avoid using your iPhone in direct sunlight or while it is charging.

3. Camera Roll Crash: This occurs when you try to access your iPhone's camera roll, and it either crashes or refuses to open. Try closing all of your apps, restarting your computer, and making sure your iPhone has the most recent software update to see if that helps.

4. No Cell Connection: Check to see whether you're within range of a cell tower and that Airplane Mode is off if you're having issues with your cellular connection. Additionally, you might try clearing the network settings in the Settings app.

5. No Wi-Fi Connection: If you're having problems connecting to Wi-Fi, make sure the network is operational and that you are within its range. Check to see if your iPhone has the newest software update, and then try restarting both your router and your iPhone.

6. Freezing or Crashed App: To force close an app, double-click the home button while swiping up on the app preview. Restarting your iPhone or uninstalling and reinstalling the app are other options.

7. Unable to update: Check your storage space and Wi-Fi connectivity if you are unable to upgrade your iPhone to the newest version. Attempt restarting your iPhone or updating it using iTunes while it is connected to a computer.

8. Camera Not Working: If your iPhone camera isn't working, try restarting your device, making sure the camera lens is clear and unobstructed, and checking that the app you're

using in the Settings app has permission to access the camera.

9. Touchscreen Not Responding: If the touchscreen on your iPhone isn't working, try forcing a restart, cleaning the screen and your hands, and checking to see if the touchscreen is being interfered with by a case.

10. Bluetooth Issues: If you're having problems connecting to a Bluetooth device, check to see if it's on, within reach, and that the iPhone's software is up-to-date. Before restarting your iPhone or Bluetooth device, make sure it is not connected to another Bluetooth device.

It's crucial to be aware of typical problems with iPhone usage as well as how to resolve them. Try the afore-mentioned advice if you run into any issues, or contact Apple Support for more help.

WHAT TO DO IF YOUR IPHONE SCREEN IS CRACKED

It might be very frustrating if your iPhone's screen is broken, but fixing it is typically a simple procedure. You can change the screen on your iPhone with the help of the following advice:

1. Assess the damage: It's important to determine the extent of the damage before having your iPhone screen replaced. If there is only a little scratch or damage, replacing the entire screen might not be necessary. However, if the screen is cracked or the touchscreen isn't functioning, a complete replacement might be necessary.
2. Backup data to iCloud: Before taking your iPhone in for repair, you must back up its data to iCloud. This will prevent you from losing any crucial data or files while the repair is being done.
3. Contact Apple for repair options: After evaluating the damage and backing up your data, you can get in touch with Apple to get the screen on your iPhone replaced. On their website, you can start by requesting an estimate. They'll then give you repair alternatives, such as shipping your device in for service or going to an Apple Store.

A professional Apple Store technician can replace your iPhone screen using genuine Apple components to ensure the performance and lifespan of your device. Apple will send you a box to mail your device to their repair facility if you choose to use their mail-in repair services. They'll mail it back to you after they've finished fixing it.

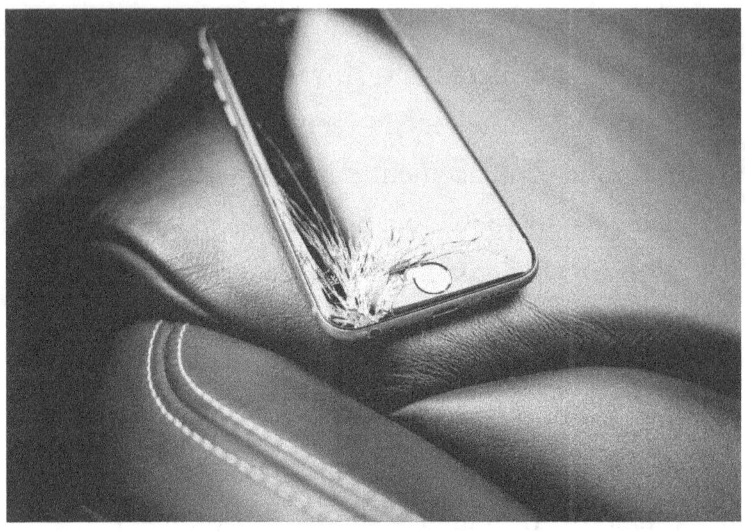

To sum up, the method of replacing the screen on your iPhone is simple. In order to acquire an estimate and make repair choices, you must first evaluate the damage, back up your data to iCloud, and then contact Apple. You can get your iPhone screen fixed quickly and easily by following these instructions.

DEALING WITH WATER DAMAGE

Water damage, which can be costly to fix, is one of the most common reasons for iPhone failure. Water damage is regrettably not covered by Apple's guarantee.

There are methods you may take to lessen the harm if your iPhone has come into contact with water or other liquids.

You should start by searching for indicators of water damage. Most iPhones include a tiny strip within the SIM card slot that, if exposed to water, will turn red or pink. If the indicator's color changes, it implies that water has entered the phone, and you need to act right away.

Use the recommended procedures for drying water-damaged phones to dry your phone. As soon as possible, turn off your iPhone and take out the SIM card tray. Then use a soft, absorbent cloth to wipe away any extra water. A hairdryer or other heat source should not be used to dry your phone, as this could cause additional damage. Instead, store your phone in a warm, dry location for at least 48 hours.

Try turning on your iPhone when the drying process is finished. Contact Apple for repair options if it won't power on or if there are still visible symptoms of water damage. Keep in mind that water damage is not covered by Apple's warranty, so you might be on the hook for the cost.

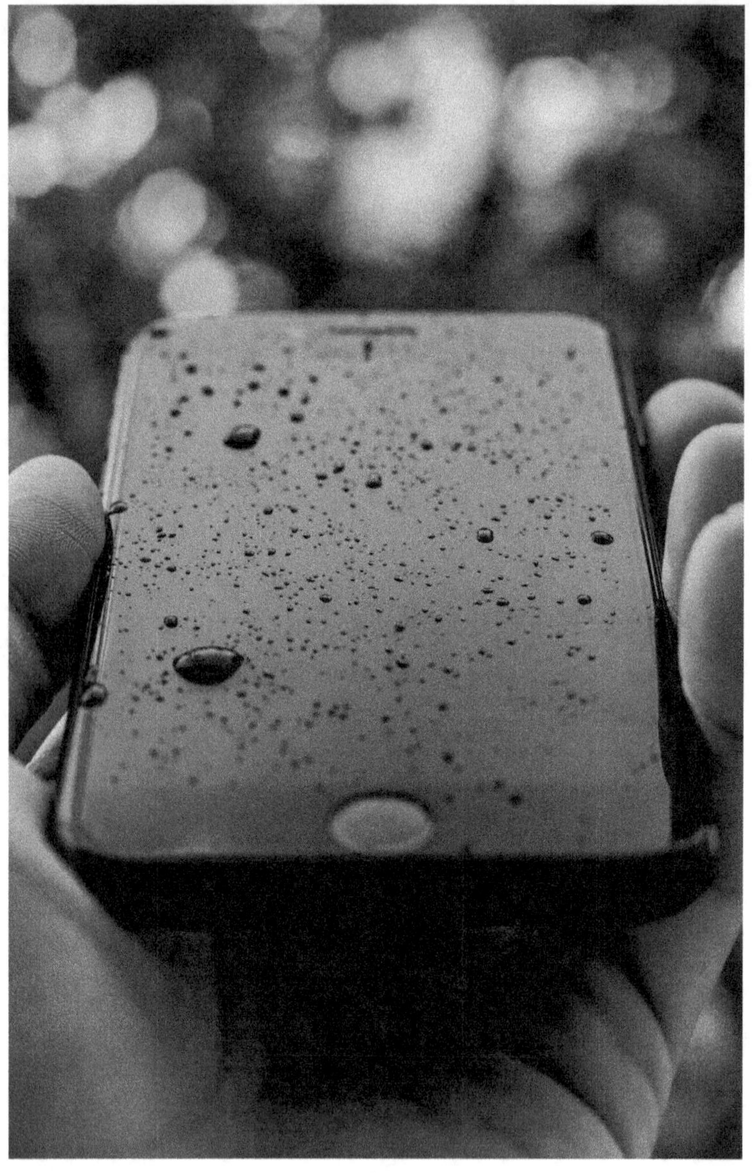

To sum up, if your iPhone gets wet, look for the water damage signal and use the best techniques for drying wet phones. Keep in mind that water damage is not covered by Apple's guarantee, so you should move quickly to reduce the damage and, if required, look into repair options.

This chapter covers common issues and faults that may arise when using iPhones and provides troubleshooting methods to resolve them. Topics discussed include freezing, overheating, Bluetooth and connectivity problems, and more. Step-by-step instructions are provided to guide readers through each issue. Tips for dealing with a cracked iPhone screen are also included. The next section is the conclusion and will tie together all the content they've covered so far.

Pass It On!

Now that you have a clear understanding of all your iPhone can do for you and how you can maximize its potential, you're in the perfect position to help someone else.

Simply by sharing your honest opinion of this book on Amazon, you'll show new readers where they can find all the information they need to make their iPhone really worth its value.

LEAVE A REVIEW!

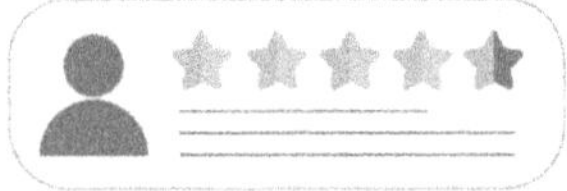

Thank you for your support. Your iPhone has a long future ahead of it!

Scan the QR code below to leave a review!

CONCLUSION

We hope that by the time we've finished our iPhone 14 tutorial, you will have a wealth of knowledge about how to make your smartphone more effective and personalized to your tastes. The possibilities of the iPhone 14 should now be well understood by you, and you should also have received thorough instructions on how to set it up and customize it to your tastes. With your new knowledge, you can now utilize all of the functions of your iPhone and have the best possible user experience.

We guided you through the crucial procedures for configuring your iPhone 14 in Chapter 1, highlighting the value of customization. We demonstrated how to personalize your device by changing the wallpaper, audio, vibration settings, and control center. In Chapter 2, we showed you how to use FaceTime, Apple's video and audio calling program, to remain in touch with your loved ones. In order to remain on top of your communications, we also gave tips on how to handle your contacts and emails efficiently and personalize your notification settings.

How to utilize your iPhone 14 to get information and use the internet was the subject of Chapter 3. We showed you how to navigate the internet, connect to websites, and quickly and simply retrieve information using Safari, the pre-installed web browser. Strategies for enhancing the productivity of your iPhone were presented in Chapter 4, "Making the Most of Your Time." You discovered how to configure Siri and how to use it successfully to finish jobs quickly and effectively. We also emphasized the significance of considering numerous aspects when utilizing Siri, such as background noise and linguistic variations.

We examined the iPhone's entertainment and leisure features in Chapter 5. We demonstrated how to utilize the Camera app to take breathtaking pictures and films that reflect your style and way of life. We also showed you how to adjust the camera settings on your iPhone to get the ideal picture. We looked at the iPhone's health and fitness capabilities in Chapter 6, including how to track your heart rate and activity levels.

The need to lock down your iPhone and safeguard your personal information was underlined in Chapter 7. We stressed the significance of setting up a strong passcode and turning on Touch ID or Face ID verification. To secure your personal information, we also suggest using the privacy tools included with the iPhone. We provide advice on how to extend the life of your iPhone's battery and how to access your iPhone's battery health recommendations in Chapter 8 to keep it functioning at its best.

Finally, we discussed some typical iPhone issues in Chapter 9 and offered useful fixes, including freezing, overheating, camera roll crashes, and connectivity problems. Making the most of your iPhone 14's features is now possible if you adhere to the directions and advice included in this book.

We hope that this guide has provided you with valuable insights and actionable advice on how to optimize your iPhone. Whether you use your iPhone for communication, entertainment, productivity, or health and fitness, this guide has something for everyone. Remember to keep your device secure and your battery healthy to ensure it stays in top condition for as long as possible. We encourage you to leave a review on Amazon and share this guide with your friends and family, who may also find it useful.

It's been a pleasure having you read this iPhone guide. We wish you the best of luck on your journey to maximizing your iPhone's potential and hope you enjoy using your device to its fullest potential.

GLOSSARY

Accessibility settings: Accessibility settings refer to the features and tools integrated into technology and digital platforms to make them more accessible to individuals with disabilities. These settings allow users to customize the interface and adjust settings to suit their unique needs.

Adjust Perspective: Adjust Perspective is a term used in photography to describe the process of manipulating the angles and composition of an image to produce a specific effect.

Airplane mode: Airplane mode is a setting on mobile devices that disables all wireless connections, including Wi-Fi, cellular data, and Bluetooth. This mode is often used during flights to comply with airline regulations and conserve battery life.

App: An app, short for application, is a software program designed to perform specific functions on a computer or mobile device. These applications might be anything from productivity tools to games.

App Sync: App Sync is a feature that automatically synchronizes data between multiple devices, allowing users to access their data from any device without manually transferring files.

App Updates: App updates refer to the latest versions of software applications that fix bugs, improve functionality, and introduce new features. From app stores or through automatic updates, users can download and install these updates.

Apple Pay: A mobile payment and digital wallet service called Apple Pay was created by Apple Inc. This service enables customers to utilize credit or debit cards kept in their digital wallet to make payments using their iPhones, iPads, or Apple Watches.

Apple Support: Apple Support is a customer support service provided by Apple Inc. to assist users with technical issues related to their products and services.

Apple user: An Apple user is someone who owns or uses Apple products, such as iPhones, iPads, Macs, or Apple Watches.

Audio-only: Audio-only refers to a media format that only includes sound and does not include visual elements such as video or images.

Auto-Brightness: Auto-brightness is a feature on mobile devices that automatically adjusts the screen's brightness based on ambient lighting conditions.

Auto-lock option: Auto-lock option is a feature on mobile devices that locks the device automatically after a specified period of inactivity.

Background App Refresh: Background App Refresh is a feature that allows apps to update their content in the background, even when the app is not actively in use. This feature can impact battery life and data usage.

Background noise: Background noise refers to any unwanted sound that is present in an audio recording, such as ambient noise or interference.

Battery Health: The capacity, effectiveness, and longevity of a mobile device's battery are all considered to be part of the battery's overall health.

Battery Life: Battery Life refers to the length of time a mobile device's battery can operate on a single charge.

Battery problems: Age, usage patterns, and software difficulties are just a few of the causes of battery troubles. Performance and battery life may be impacted by these issues.

Battery Usage: Battery Usage refers to the amount of power consumed by a mobile device's battery while in use, including the usage of apps and other features.

QR code: Quick Response codes, or QR codes, are two-dimensional barcodes that may be scanned by mobile devices to access information or carry out particular tasks.

Bluetooth: With the help of Bluetooth, devices may communicate wirelessly and exchange data across short distances. Commonly, this technology is used to link mobile devices to other gadgets like speakers, head-phones, and automobiles.

Brightness and sharpness settings: Brightness and sharpness settings are visual display options that allow users to adjust the brightness and sharpness of their iPhone's screen.

Call link: A call link is a feature that allows users to initiate a phone call directly from a website or email. This feature is often used in business settings to enable quick and easy communication between customers and service providers.

Camera timer: Camera timer is a feature that allows users to set a delay timer before taking a photo with their iPhone's camera. This feature is useful for taking group photos or self-portraits.

Cellular network: Cellular network is a wireless communication system that enables mobile devices to connect to the internet and other mobile devices via radio waves.

Connectivity issues: Connectivity issues refer to any problems encountered when trying to establish or maintain a network or internet connection on an iPhone.

Control Center: Control Center is a feature on an iPhone that allows users to quickly access and adjust settings, such as brightness, volume, and airplane mode, from a single location.

Crashing: Crashing is an issue that occurs when an app suddenly stops working or closes unexpectedly on an iPhone.

Cropping and rotation: Cropping and rotation are editing tools available on an iPhone that allow users to modify the size, aspect ratio, and orientation of images and videos.

Data consumption: Data consumption refers to the amount of data used by an iPhone when browsing the internet, using apps, or performing other online activities.

Dictation: Dictation is a feature on an iPhone that allows users to dictate spoken words or phrases, which are then converted into text. This feature can be used for various tasks, such as sending messages or composing emails, without the need for typing.

Dim Screen: Dim Screen is set on an iPhone that allows users to adjust the brightness of the screen, potentially saving battery life while making it more comfortable for the eyes to use the device in low-light conditions.

Disabling camera noise: Disabling camera noise refers to the ability of an iPhone user to silence the shutter sound that is typically made when taking a photo or recording a video, which can be helpful in situations where silence is preferred.

Display and Privacy Controls: Display and Privacy Controls are settings that allow iPhone users to customize how their personal information and device are presented and shared with others. This includes control over app permissions, location sharing, and other privacy-related settings.

Electrocardiogram (ECG): Electrocardiogram (ECG) is a feature available on some iPhone models that allows users to measure their heart rate and rhythm through electrical sensors on the device.

Exposure: Exposure is a camera setting on an iPhone that determines how much light is let into the camera's sensor, allowing for adjustments in brightness and contrast to create the desired photographic effect.

Face ID: Face ID is a facial recognition feature on an iPhone that uses advanced technology to identify and authenticate the device's user, allowing for secure access to apps, payment services, and other features.

FaceTime: FaceTime is an Apple-made app that allows iPhone users to make voice and video calls with other Apple device users over the internet with high-quality audio and video.

Filter: Filter is an editing tool available on an iPhone that allows users to modify the color and appearance of photos and videos, creating different visual effects and moods.

Find My: Find My is a feature on an iPhone that allows users to locate their device, as well as other Apple devices that are linked to their iCloud account, if they are lost or stolen.

Fitness: Fitness refers to the collection of health and exercise-related features available on an iPhone, including step tracking, workout monitoring, and other tools designed to promote physical activity and healthy living.

Freezing: When an iPhone freezes, it becomes unresponsive or non-functional and may be due to a hardware problem, a software bug, or other problems.

Genuine Apple components: Genuine Apple components are replacement parts and accessories that are made and certified by Apple, ensuring compatibility, quality, and safety.

Geo-tagging photos: Geo-tagging photos is a feature available on an iPhone that adds geographic location data to photos, allowing users to keep track of where their photos were taken and to create location-based albums.

Hardware problems: Hardware problems refer to issues with the physical components of an iPhone, such as a cracked screen, malfunctioning buttons, or a broken charging port.

Hide My Email: Hide My Email is a feature available on an iPhone that allows users to create a temporary email address for online forms and other purposes, providing an additional layer of privacy and security.

Home screen: The Home screen is the main screen of an iPhone, where users can access their apps, widgets, and other important features.

iCloud: Apple's cloud-based storage service, known as iCloud, enables iPhone owners to access their files and data from any internet-connected device.

iCloud Backup: iCloud Backup is a feature on an iPhone that automatically backs up data and settings to iCloud, allowing users to restore their device's content if it is lost, damaged, or replaced.

Internet connection: An iPhone's capacity to connect to and use the internet, whether via cellular data or a Wi-Fi network, is referred to as having an internet connection. Many iPhone features and functions require a steady and dependable internet connection.

iOS: an operating system for mobile devices developed by Apple Inc. and only available for iPhones.

iPadOS: An operating system specifically designed for use on Apple's iPad devices.

Keychain: a solution for securely storing and managing passwords for numerous websites and apps on iOS devices.

Live photos: A feature on iPhones that allows users to take a still photo that also captures a few seconds of video and audio.

Location Services: A feature on iPhones that allows apps to access the device's location information to provide location-based services.

Lock screen control: An iPhone feature that enables users to access specific controls and features from the lock screen, such as the camera or music player.

Low Power Mode: An iPhone setting that lowers power usage by turning off several features and background processes.

macOS: A desktop operating system created by Apple Inc. that runs on Mac computers.

Maximum Capacity: A measure of the maximum amount of charge an iPhone battery can hold compared to its original capacity.

Medical ID: an iPhone feature that lets users generate emergency medical ID cards that can be accessed from the lock screen.

Metrics: Data collected and analyzed to provide insights into the performance and usage of an iPhone.

Mirror front camera: A feature on iPhones that flips the front-facing camera image to create a mirror image.

Mirroring: A feature on iPhones that allows users to mirror the device's screen onto an external display.

Natural language processing: A technology used on iPhones to analyze and understand human language and communicate with users in a natural way.

Network settings: Settings on an iPhone that control how the device connects to the internet and other networks.

Passcode lock: A security feature on iPhones that demands a passcode be entered in order to open the gadget.

Peak Performance Capability messages: Messages on iPhones that alert users when the device's performance is being managed to prevent unexpected shutdowns.

Performance Management: A feature on iPhones that manages the device's performance to prevent unexpected shutdowns.

Photo Editor: iPhones include a built-in app that users may use to edit and improve their images.

Portrait mode: A camera feature on iPhones that creates a blurred background effect to highlight the subject of the photo.

Private Browsing: A mode on Safari, the default web browser on iPhones, that prevents browsing history and other data from being saved.

Productivity tool: An app or feature on an iPhone designed to increase productivity and efficiency, such as a to-do list or calendar app.

Push Notifications: Notifications that appear on an iPhone's lock screen or in the notification center to alert users of new messages, updates, or other events.

Raise to Wake: A feature on iPhones that wakes up the device's screen when the user picks up the phone.

Resetting camera settings: A process that restores the iPhone's camera settings to their default values.

Restarting: Turning an iPhone off and back on again to resolve performance issues or other problems.

Safari: The default web browser on iPhones, developed by Apple Inc.

Settings: A system on the iPhone that allows users to customize and configure various aspects of their device, such as wireless networks, notifications, privacy settings, and more.

Sharing Links: The ability to easily share URLs or links to websites or content via various channels, such as messaging apps or email.

Siri: An intelligent personal assistant that responds to voice commands and queries from iPhone users, providing assistance with various tasks such as setting reminders, sending messages, and answering questions.

Smart Search Bar: A feature on the iPhone that provides suggestions and quick access to frequently visited websites, bookmarks, and search history.

Software bugs: Errors or flaws in the software code of the iPhone that can cause issues with performance, stability, or functionality.

Third-party apps: Applications developed by entities other than Apple that can be downloaded and installed on the iPhone to provide additional functionality or services.

Touch ID: A biometric authentication system that allows users to unlock their iPhone or authorize purchases by scanning their fingerprint.

Tricorder: A fictional device from the Star Trek franchise that has inspired real-world technology, including various iPhone apps that function as medical diagnostic tools.

Troubleshooting: The process of identifying and resolving issues or problems that arise with the iPhone, such as performance issues, network connectivity problems, or software bugs.

Virtual assistant: A digital assistant that uses artificial intelligence to perform various tasks or provide information to users via natural language commands or queries.

Vital indications: Health-related metrics, such as heart rate, blood pressure, or oxygen saturation, that can be measured or monitored using various iPhone apps or accessories.

Voice commands: Spoken instructions that turn on various iPhone functions or services, such as placing phone calls, sending messages, or setting reminders.

watchOS: The operating system used on Apple Watch devices, allowing users to monitor their health and fitness, access apps, and receive notifications on their wrists.

Widgets: Miniature apps or tools that can be added to the iPhone's home screen or notification center, providing quick access to information or features without needing to open a full app.

REFERENCES

Aguilar, N. (2022, September 20). *Here's How to Set Up Your New iPhone 14*. CNET. https://www.cnet.com/tech/mobile/heres-how-to-set-up-your-new-iphone-14/

Chan, C., & published, A. O. (2021, December 25). *How to set up your new iPhone*. IMore. https://www.imore.com/how-set-your-new-iphone

Change iPhone sounds and vibrations. (n.d.). Apple Support. https://support.apple.com/en-ca/guide/iphone/iph07c867f28/ios

Connect to Wi-Fi on your iPhone, iPad, or iPod touch. (n.d.). Apple Support. https://support.apple.com/en-ca/HT202639

Everything You Need to Know About the Apple Health App. (2022, February 22). Lifewire. https://www.lifewire.com/apple-health-app-4691255

Fiaz, H. (2017, May 10). *A Complete Guide to Your iPhone's Health App and How to Use It*. MUO. https://www.makeuseof.com/tag/making-sense-iphone-health-app/

Gil, L. (2019, September 3). *How to create a new Apple ID on your iPhone or iPad*. iMore. https://www.imore.com/how-create-new-apple-id-your-iphone-or-ipad

Imran, S. (2022, June 24). *What Is iCloud and What Can You Use It For?* MUO. https://www.makeuseof.com/what-is-icloud/

iPhone Basics: Security and General Settings. (n.d.). GCFGlobal.org. https://edu.gcfglobal.org/en/iphonebasics/security-and-general-settings/1/

iPhone Battery and Performance. (n.d.). Apple Support. https://support.apple.com/en-ca/HT208387

iPhone camera basics. (n.d.). Apple Support. https://support.apple.com/en-ca/guide/iphone/iph263472f78/ios

Paiker, N. (n.d.). *21 Most Popular iPhone Problems and How to Fix Them*.

Stellarinfo.com. https://www.stellarinfo.com/article/fix-iPhone-problems.php

Phungglan, J. (n.d.). *iPhone Camera settings you should be using for better photos.* MacPaw. https://macpaw.com/how-to/iphone-camera-settings

Set up Messages on iPhone. (n.d.). Apple Support. https://support.apple.com/en-ca/guide/iphone/iph3d039b67/ios

Shah, P. (2021, December 3). *6 Best Ways to Manage Notifications on iPhone.* Guiding Tech. https://www.guidingtech.com/best-ways-to-manage-notifications-on-iphone/

Thakur, A. (2022, August 19). *How to customize alert and notification sounds on your iPhone.* IDownloadBlog.com. https://www.idownloadblog.com/2022/08/19/how-to-customize-alert-sounds-on-iphone/

Top 25 sharing knowledge quotes. (n.d.). A-Z Quotes. Retrieved May 20, 2023, from https://www.azquotes.com/tag/sharing-knowledge

Turn on and set up iPhone. (n.d.). Apple Support. https://support.apple.com/en-ca/guide/iphone/iph1fd7e482f/ios

Two-factor authentication for Apple ID. (n.d.). Apple Support. https://support.apple.com/en-ca/HT204915

Updated, L. F. from N. R. last. (2016, September 13). *How to create and customize vibration alerts on your iPhone.* IMore. https://www.imore.com/how-set-custom-alert-vibrations-or-disable-them-your-iphone-and-ipad

Wesson, K. (2019, October 28). *How To Edit Photos On iPhone Using The Built-In Photos App.* IPhone Photography School. https://iphonephotographyschool.com/how-to-edit-photos-on-iphone/

Whitney, L. (2022, December 21). *How to Use and Customize the Control Center on Your iPhone or iPad.* PCMAG. https://www.pcmag.com/how-to/how-to-use-customize-control-center-on-your-iphone-or-ipad

IMAGE REFERENCE

Bhattacharya, A. (2019). *Water Droplets on iPhone* [Image]. Unsplash. https://unsplash.com/photos/zTT3FI63M_Q

Binay, O. (2021). *Young man playing PUBG Mobile with iPhone* [Image]. Unsplash. https://unsplash.com/photos/cQ90QkreiPQ

Bradley, T. (2020). [Image]. Unsplash. https://unsplash.com/photos/ap8jsn3B9gI

Chystiakov, E. (2023). *Video production* [Image]. Unsplash. https://unsplash.com/photos/OUits4XmNkU

Du Preez, P. (2020). *Calender* [Image]. Unsplash. https://unsplash.com/photos/JbAv3nAKOtc

Fewings, N. (2020). *Checking the direction of a cruise ship in Bournemouth Bay, using the Compass App on an IPhone* [Image]. Unsplash. https://unsplash.com/photos/lirOPuejTbM

Hudson, D. (2020). *September 2020 planner and techy tools tools* [Image]. Unsplash. https://unsplash.com/photos/LXWUK-gypVc

Jordan, B. (2020a & b). *Iphone, ios, home screen, close up, pixels, retina, smartphone, icon, ios 14, icon, screen, phone, music, itunes, songs* [Image]. Unsplash. https://unsplash.com/photos/IHecRXio89c

Jordan, B. (2020c). Blue and White Google Chrome Logo [Image]. Unsplash. https://www.pexels.com/photo/blue-and-white-google-chrome-logo-5426403/

Jordan, B. (2020d). *Settings* [Image]. Unsplash. https://www.pexels.com/photo/iphone-smartphone-app-i-os-5437583/

Jordan, B. (2020e). *Blue and White Logo Guessing Game* [Image]. Unsplash. https://www.pexels.com/photo/blue-and-white-logo-guessing-game-5444628/

Lastovich, T. (2017). *Black Iphone 7 on Brown Table* [Image]. Unsplash. https://www.pexels.com/photo/black-iphone-7-on-brown-table-699122/

Matoo Studio. (2023). *Netflix logo on an iPhone screen. A TV set with the profiles selection screen.* [Image]. Unsplash. https://unsplash.com/photos/3qdNESbMrjk

Mistry, A. (2022). *Download this HD iphone wallpaper* [Image]. Unsplash. https://unsplash.com/photos/OI58xzlEZkw

Nguyen, T. (2022). *Apple iPhone 14 Purple* [Image]. Unsplash. https://unsplash.com/photos/nxo1dv5tkmo

Picjumbo.com. (2016). *Space Gray Iphone 6* [Image]. Unsplash. https://www.pexels.com/photo/space-gray-iphone-6-196653/

Samkov, I. (2020). *Person Having a Video Call* [Image]. Unsplash. https://www.pexels.com/photo/person-having-a-video-call-4240608/

Serban, V. (2022). *iPhone on box* [Image]. Unsplash. https://unsplash.com/photos/H-mzalaeXYU

Shah, M. (2023). *Phone charging* [Image]. Pixabay. https://pixabay.com/images/id-7832257/

Tran Mau Tri Tam. (2021). *Make paying easier with wallet* [Image]. Unsplash. https://unsplash.com/photos/3xFwO_wTrkg

Yao, R. (2018). *An iPhone with dark wallpaper and a black headphone* [Image]. Unsplash. https://unsplash.com/photos/OxJfpSlZOu0